STO

ACPL ITEM
DISCARD S0-AUH-606

AUG 15 '74

THE LABOUR GOVERNMENT AND BRITISH INDUSTRY
1945–1951

THE LABOUR GOVERNMENT AND BRITISH INDUSTRY 1945–1951

By A. A. ROGOW

With the Assistance of
PETER SHORE

GREENWOOD PRESS, PUBLISHERS
WESTPORT, CONNECTICUT

Library of Congress Cataloging in Publication Data

Rogow, Arnold A
   The Labour government and British industry, 1945-
1951.

   Reprint of the 1955 ed. published by Cornell Univer-
sity Press, Ithaca, N. Y.
   Includes bibliographical references.
   1. Great Britain--Economic policy. I. Title.
[HC256.5.R65 1974]   338.942   73-22508
ISBN 0-8371-6374-9

DEDICATION

For Kate and Jenny

Originally published in 1955 by Cornell University Press,
Ithaca, New York

Reprinted with permission of A.A. Rogow and the
Right Honourable Peter Shore, M.P.

Reprinted in 1974 by Greenwood Press,
a division of Williamhouse-Regency Inc.

Library of Congress Catalog Card Number 73-22508

ISBN 0-8371-6374-9

Printed in the United States of America

1807522

CONTENTS

A SEMI-REVOLUTION

I advocate a semi-revolution.
The trouble with a total revolution
(Ask any reputable Rosicrucian)
Is that it brings the same class up on top.
Executives of skilful execution
Will therefore plan to go half-way and stop.
Yes, revolutions are the only salves,
But they're one thing that should be done by halves.

ROBERT FROST.

A TOTAL REVOLUTION
(*An Answer for Robert Frost*)

I advocate a total revolution.
The trouble with a semi-revolution,
It's likely to be slow as evolution.
Who wants to spend the ages in collusion
With Compromise, Complacence and Confusion?
As for the same class coming up on top
That's wholecloth from the propaganda shop ;
The old saw says there's loads of room on top,
That's where the poor should really plan to stop.
And speaking of those people called the ' haves ',
Who own the whole cow and must have the calves
(And plant the wounds so they can sell the salves)
They won't be stopped by doing things by halves.
I say that for a permanent solution
There's nothing like a total revolution!

P.S.   And may I add by way of a conclusion
      I wouldn't dream to ask a Rosicrucian.

OSCAR WILLIAMS.

PREFACE

Like most writers of books based on extensive research I am indebted to a large number of individuals and organizations for various kinds of assistance. I cannot mention all of them in this brief space, but I am nevertheless deeply grateful for their contribution to these pages. I should like to acknowledge a special debt to the Social Science Research Council, Washington, D.C., whose provision of a fellowship made possible the research. I owe much to Professors William Ebenstein and H. H. Wilson, Princeton University, for stimulation and encouragement at every stage.

I should like to express thanks to the research and secretarial staffs of the following organizations: Labour Party; Conservative Party; Liberal Party; Transport and General Workers Union; Fabian Society; Political and Economic Planning; Industrial Welfare Society; Aims of Industry; Iron and Steel Federation; and Federation of British Industries.

I am grateful to Thomas Balogh for a number of valuable comments and criticisms, and I should also like to acknowledge the assistance of the following: N. Barou; R. H. S. Crossman, O.B.E., M.P.; the Rt. Hon. Clement Davies P.C., M.P.; Dame Alix Gilroy; Sir Oscar Hobson; Isobel Jarvis; Norman Mackenzie; John Marsh; James Stewart Martin; Kingsley Martin; T. E. M. McKitterick; Graeme C. Moodie; E. Hulbert-Powell; Colonel R. A. C. Radcliffe; Paul Rykens; Sir Cecil M. Weir, K.C.M.G., K.B.E.; and Mrs. Helen Wright.

My greatest debt is to my friend, Peter Shore. His suggestions had a considerable influence on the research design, and many of his ideas, in whole or in part, were incorporated in the writing. In addition, it was he who undertook to prepare the manuscript for publication. He, therefore, deserves equal credit with me for whatever merit the book possesses.

But I alone am responsible for errors of fact, opinion, and interpretation. I do not expect that the individuals and organizations mentioned will agree with all, or even with any, of the evaluations set forth, but I hope that they will find them worthy of consideration.

Finally, I should mention that portions of the book have appeared in articles in the following journals : *Public Opinion Quarterly, Journal of Politics, New Statesman and Nation, American Journal of Economics and Sociology, Canadian Journal of Economics and Political Science.*

ARNOLD A. ROGOW.

Stanford, California,
April 5, 1955.

CHAPTER I

INTRODUCTION

Revolutions, like governments, take their character from the people. For almost three hundred years social change in Britain has come about through peaceful means and with a minimum of violence, and the British, above all else, are a peaceful and non-violent people. Argumentativeness rather than quarrelsomeness ; an ability to resolve clashes of interest or class without suppression of conflicting groups ; a tendency to apply intelligence to problems, although not always to produce intelligent solutions— these are the enduring characteristics of the British people and of the political instruments they have forged. In the last two centuries a transfer of power from the landed aristocracy to the middle classes, and, more recently, a further, if partial, transfer of power to the working classes, has been accomplished, not merely without force or bloodshed, but without erosion of the basic ethics and customs of a parliamentary democracy. In this, British society has almost no parallel in time. Indeed, in a declining age of reason and a dawning era of irrationality and violence, Britain is a last bright symbol of enlightenment.

This study was conceived as an attempt to explore the significance of the most recent British revolution ; the achievement of the Labour Government from 1945 to 1951. Of a number of possible approaches the one chosen was that which, in the opinion of the writer, was likely to throw the most light on the substantive impact of the Labour Government, namely, the relations between the Labour Government and British industry. Such a study, it was thought, would provide tentative answers to a number of questions ; (1) Was the 1945-51 revolution a genuine revolution ; that is, was there a substantial transfer of power from the middle to the working classes? (2) To what extent did the displaced groups, primarily business or business-related, co-operate with the Labour Government, and on what terms? (3) Where there was conflict between Government and industry, how did business opposition manifest itself, in general and in

B

particular? (4) Was the Labour Government able to influence, to any considerable extent, the structure, psychology, and objectives of British industry? The answers to these questions, it was believed, would also illuminate the character of the modern Welfare State; for it is probable that future Welfare States, in the United States and elsewhere, will be patterned after the British experience. Finally, in so far as the study is concerned with problems of change in society, it suggests some questions which must be faced by reformers in any democratic society. To what extent can reform in practice realise postulated objectives? Is the empirical approach to social reconstruction— 'playing by ear' someone has termed it—a satisfactory substitute for reform based on ideology or theory? Does limited reform, by making conditions more tolerable, reduce the need for radical reform, and if so, how is a reform movement to remain both dynamic and popular? These are some of the challenges which confronted British Labour, and which still must be resolved. The writer's own views, set forth in the last chapter of the study, present a tentative assessment of the problems stated, with reference to the Labour Government experiment.

Initially, however, it is important to discuss in some detail Labour's own conception of its task in 1945. Too often, on both sides of the Atlantic, the Labour Government is criticised not for what it failed to achieve, but for what it failed to *want* to achieve. Clearly, Britain to-day, measured by Marxist or Utopian socialist standards, is not a socialist society, and this is sometimes taken to prove that the Labour Government failed to establish socialism. Of course it failed, but assuredly it never set out to create either a New Russia or a New Lanark. Although the issues of present-day British politics are couched in terms of socialism versus capitalism, equality versus privilege, the workers versus the 'bosses', and so on, the rhetoric of the political campaign does not necessarily connect with the raw facts of politics. In point of fact, the policy of neither of the major parties is characterised by purity of doctrine. Thus, in 1945 the policies and programme of the Labour Government were, to a large extent, inherited from the war time, Conservative-dominated Coalition Government, and similarly, the present Conservative Government has retained intact most of the legislative changes wrought by its predecessor. The point of departure, therefore, must be an attempt to break through semantics into the area of effective policy and approach; to determine first of all, what the Labour Government conceived to be its programme in 1945, and in terms of this programme to evaluate results.

The 1945 programme, of course, did not spring full-blown from the inner sanctum of the Party headquarters on Election day.[1] In its essentials it followed the proposals of the almost thirty-year-old historic policy statement, *Labour and the New Social Order*, which, in 1918, for the first time committed the Party to extensive nationalisation of industry and redistribution of income. While through the intervening years the 1918 policy statement had been elaborated by Party conferences, and the writings of influential individuals,[2] as a statement of policy it remained fundamentally unaltered. Its key proposals—nationalisation of public utilities and certain natural resources, public control of industry, egalitarian taxation—were incorporated and adumbrated in the 1945 statement, *Let Us Face the Future*.[3]

It is significant that the first point taken up by the 1945 policy statement is civil liberties. The Labour Party, it declares,

> stands for freedom—for freedom of worship, freedom of speech, freedom of the Press. The Labour Party will see to it that we keep and enlarge these freedoms, and that we enjoy again the personal civil liberties we have, of our own free will, sacrificed to win the war.

On the other hand,

> there are certain so-called freedoms that Labour will not

[1] Statements of policy and objectives will be found in the various publications of the Labour Party, particularly the policy statements and manifestoes, and in the following: Clement Attlee, *Purpose and Policy: Collected Speeches* (London, 1946); ... *Labour Party in Perspective and 12 years Later* (London, 1949); Lord Latham and others, *What Labour Could Do* (Fabian Society Lectures, London, 1945); John Parker, *Labour Marches On* (London, 1947); Douglas Jay, *The Socialist Case* (London, 1947); Michael Young, *Labour's Plan for Plenty* (London, 1947); Francis Williams, *Socialist Britain* (New York, 1949); Aneurin Bevan *In Place of Fear* (New York, 1952); R. H. S. Crossman, ed. *New Fabian Essays* (London, 1952).

[2] See, for example, Cripps and others, *Problems of a Socialist Government* (London, 1933); Herbert Morrison, *Socialisation and Transport* (London, 1933); Ernest Bevin, *The Job to Be Done* (London, 1942).

[3] *Let Us Face the Future* (London, April, 1945).

tolerate ; freedom to exploit other people ; freedom to pay poor wages and to push up prices for selfish profits ; freedom to deprive the people of the means of living full, happy, healthy lives.

The nation, it was noted, needed a ' tremendous overhaul ' including the modernisation and re-equipment of homes, schools, social services, and industry. While all parties admitted the need, only the Labour Party was

> prepared to achieve it by drastic policies of replanning and by keeping a firm constructive hand on our whole productive machinery . . . Labour will plan from the group up—giving an appropriate place to constructive enterprise and private endeavour in the national plan, but dealing decisively with those interests which would use high-sounding talk about economic freedom to cloak their determination to put themselves and their wishes above those of the whole nation.

As set forth in *Let Us Face the Future*, the Labour Party was committed to full employment in almost absolute terms.

> Full employment in any case, and if we need to keep a firm public hand on industry in order to get jobs for all, very well . . . The price of so-called ' economic freedom ' for the few is too high if it is bought at the cost of idleness and misery for millions.

Full employment, it was suggested, would be achieved through partial nationalisation of industry, the full utilisation of national resources; the provision of good wages, social services and insurance ; tax policy, and planned investment.

Nationalisation of industry, it was clear, would affect only those ' basic industries ripe and over-ripe for public ownership and management ', defined as the fuel and power industries, inland transport (rail, road, air, and canal), and the iron and steel industry. Smaller businesses ' can be left to go on with their useful work ' and basic industries ' not yet ripe for public ownership ' would be subject to ' constructive supervision ', including the control of monopolies and cartels, the ' shaping of suitable economic and price controls' and a 'firm and clear-cut programme for the export trade'.

Subsequent policy statements added little to this enumeration of policy towards industry. The principal addition in *Let Us Win Through Together*,[1] the 1950 policy statement, was the listing of the sugar, cement, 'appropriate sections' of the chemical, 'all suitable minerals', water, cold storage, meat importing and wholesaling, and insurance industries as suitable for nationalisation, and the announcement that Development Councils for industry, 'on which management, workers and the public are represented will be set up, compulsorily if need be'. The policy statement, *Labour and the New Society*,[2] issued after the 1950 General Election which returned Labour with a narrow majority of six seats, did not contain a list of industries proposed for nationalisation, but presented, for the first time, three 'tests' by which the suitability of an industry for nationalisation could be determined. These were : if it was an industry ' on which the economic life and welfare of the community depend . . . (and which) cannot be left safely in the hands of groups of private owners not answerable to the community ' ; if it was inefficient ; and if it was a monopoly. Basic controls over private industry were defined as controls over investment, monopoly, foreign exchange, and factory location ; limitation of dividends and encouragement of re-investment of profits ; and the provision of technical and scientific aid by Government. As still another means of control, public enterprises, it was stated,

> will be set up to compete fairly and squarely with private firms which are not pulling their weight in the national effort. This will provide a spur to greater efficiency and a weapon against monopoly.

A discussion of the other sections of the policy statements, mainly concerned with foreign affairs and the social services, is outside the scope of this study. They are synthesised, however, together with those aspects of the programme that have been examined, in what the Labour Party regarded as the ultimate

[1] *Let Us Win Through Together* (London, January 1950).
[2] *Labour and the New Society* (London, August, 1950).

ends of policy, the broad objectives for which it was striving.
If the Party's statements of philosophy can be taken literally, then
there is no doubt that the Labour Party's

> ultimate purpose at home is the establishment of a Socialist
> Commonwealth of Great Britain—free, democratic, efficient,
> progressive, public spirited, its material resources organised
> in the service of the British people.[1]

As put by Harold Laski in 1948, the Labour Party was

> trying to transform a profoundly bourgeois society, mainly
> composed of what Bagehot called 'deferential' citizens,
> allergic to theory because long centuries of success have
> trained it to distrust of philosophic speculation, and acquies-
> cent in the empiricist's dogma that somehow something is
> bound to turn up, a society, moreover, in which all the
> major criteria of social values have been imposed by a long
> indoctrination for whose aid all the power of church and
> school, of press and cinema, have been very skilfully mobil-
> ised ; we have got to transform this bourgeois society into a
> socialist society, with foundations not less secure than those
> it seeks to renovate.[2]

The achievement between 1945 and 1951 fell short of these
stated goals. The essence of the Labour Government's accomplishment was the creation of a mixed economy with the means of
production largely under private ownership, and with the provision of greater opportunity for individual advancement.

It would be unfair, however, to suggest that the Labour Party
betrayed either its hopes or its promises. In the first place, the
'gradualist' approach to social change, which was first identified
with Fabian Socialism, has long been a central conception of
Party doctrine. Thus the 1945 programme was designed not to
achieve Socialism at once, but to take the first steps toward the
creation of a Socialist society. It was broadly recognised, for
example, that the customs, conventions and machinery of Parliament, which assigned the Opposition an important role in debate,

---

[1] *Let Us Face the Future*, p. 6.
[2] Harold Laski, ' Efficiency in **Government**,' *The Road to Recovery* (Fabian Society
Lectures, London, 1948), p. 50.

initially limited the scope and amount of legislation. It is also true that many of the Government's measures, particularly with reference to nationalisation, were regarded as experimental, to be tried and tested over a period of time before further progress was attempted. While the establishment of the ' Socialist Commonwealth' remained the goal of Party policy, the pragmatic approach was not discarded but invoked periodically to assess the practical achievement. The ultimate objective, it was clear, would in turn be shaped by examination of the interim results.

It is also important that the Labour Government proceeded without reference to any particular theory other than pragmatism, and for that reason lacked any precise conception of Socialism or of social change. Whether or not, in the words of R. H. S. Crossman,

> this absence of a theoretical basis for practical programmes of action is the main reason why the post-war Labour Government marked the end of a century of social reform and not, as its socialist supporters had hoped, the beginning of a new epoch,[1]

the lack of theory was to some extent responsible for incomplete results. Within the Labour Party the conscious articulation of Socialist principles has always been the concern of a relatively small number of individuals, chiefly intellectuals and Fabians. Although, to quote the 1945 Policy Statement, the ' Labour Party is a Socialist Party, and proud of it ', the majority of its members tend to accept the characterisation without, however, defining its meaning, and certainly without careful scrutiny of the general programme from a Socialist point of view. Consequently, at any given moment the Party contains extremists, moderates, and essentially liberal reformers, who may be united on specific policies but who will differ on theoretical approach. In this confusion of theory and practice, of ideas and interests, which is a feature of any Labour Party Conference, social policies are often mistaken for Socialism ; or to put it another way, certain policies which, elsewhere, have been associated with New Deals, Popular

[1] R. H. S. Crossman, ' Towards a Philosophy of Socialism,' in Crossman, ed., *New Fabian Essays*, pp. 5–6.

Fronts, or Liberal Parties, have been associated with Socialism and the Labour Party in Britain.

It remains true, of course, that a theory of Democratic Socialism can be developed from the policies of the Labour Government, and in fact, the world Socialist movement issued in 1951 a statement of principles which was based, in large part, on the British achievement.[1] The International Socialist Conference which met at Frankfurt in June–July, 1951, declared that while different forms of Socialism are possible, Democratic Socialism differs from Communism in that it admits the right of opposition and the existence of more than one political party. Socialist planning, it held, does not presuppose public ownership of all the means of production, but it is essential that the State prevent private owners from abusing their powers. The Conference further maintained that economic power should be decentralized wherever compatible with planning, and it insisted that ' the workers must be associated democratically with the direction of their industry '.[2]

As elaborated by the Labour Government 1945–51, the theory assumes that where industry is nationalised the State, rather than guild or syndicalist organisations, is to exercise control. So far as the private sector of industry is concerned, control is to be effected less by direction than by establishing the environment in which industry is to operate, particularly with reference to supply and demand factors.[3] The remaining principal responsibilities of the State are full employment, the provision of security through State-aided health, education, and insurance schemes, and fiscal policies aimed at achieving a more egalitarian distribution of income.

So stated, the theory has much in common with general theories of planning, and, indeed, it has been suggested that the

---

[1] Noting that the background of the Conference was the post-war achievements of Labour Governments in Britain, New Zealand, Australia, Sweden, and Norway, the *Times* commented editorially, July 2, 1951, that ' this statement is a rationalisation of the way in which they have found themselves behaving.'

[2] This account of the Conference's ' Declaration of Principles ' is based on a report in *The Times*, July 2, 1951.

[3] This aspect of Socialist theory is elaborated in W. Arthur Lewis, *The Principles of Economic Planning*. (A Study prepared for the Fabian Society, London, 1949), pp. 12–22.

achievement of the Labour Government was not Socialism but 'merely welfare capitalism', because

(i) Though the national income is rather more fairly distributed than before, the concentration of capital and so of economic privilege remains unchanged.

(ii) Profits, wages and salaries are still determined not by any conditions of national interest or social justice, but by the traditional methods of *laisser-faire*. Under conditions of full employment, this must result in a continuous inflationary pressure, which undermines the real value of social security and small savings, as well as making our products less competitive in foreign markets and so jeopardizing our capacity to maintain the standard of living.

(iii) Though certain basic industries are transformed into public corporations and private industry is subject to some control, effective power remains in the hands of a small managerial and Civil Service élite.

. . . The main task of Socialism to-day is to prevent the concentration of power in the hands of *either* industrial management *or* the state bureaucracy—in brief, to distribute responsibility and so to enlarge freedom of choice.[1]

But it is not quite fair to maintain that 'This task was not even begun by the Labour Government.'[2] In the first place, nationalisation itself, whether or not the former managers continued in power, represented a substantial transfer of responsibility in the simple fact of State ownership. It is also important that through the provision of full employment, a distribution of the national income in favour of the wage-earner, and the creation of opportunity, some freedom of choice for the first time became a reality for large numbers of citizens. It would be more fair to suggest, in short, that the task was begun but not completed, and as this study attempts to demonstrate, that in certain areas a new start or approach is required. But it cannot be seriously doubted, whatever term is applied to the accomplishment, that much was achieved by the Labour Government, and while much more remains to be done, the British experiment in democratic planning

[1] Crossman, op. cit., pp. 26–27.   [2] ibid., p. 27.

between 1945 and 1951 set a standard for the West that will not soon be surpassed. To British citizens, of course, the political scene is no great puzzle. It is broadly recognised, even in the heat of an election campaign, that the Conservatives if elected will not bring back the *laisser-faire* of the Victorian era, and that Labour will not achieve the nightmare of Orwell's *1984*. The British, it may be said, are at home with a lack of theory, and do well enough with the confusion of terminology that bewilders foreigners. In the main, the British understand by the term Labour more planning and control, and by the term Conservative, less. It may be speculated that an era of peace and abundance would sharpen differences between the parties, and that, for instance, a Conservative Government would severely restrict the role of the State, if the situation permitted. For the present and immediate future, however, uncertain world conditions will continue to determine the conditions of life in Britain, and hence the scope of Government. In this context, where the issue of national survival is paramount to other considerations, neither Party can afford devotion to ideology.

In assessing the relations between the Labour Government and industry, therefore, this study will proceed on the assumption that the Labour Government set out to create a society with the following basic features : (1) nationalisation of basic industries ; (2) effective public control of business ; (3) relative social equality and security ; (4) transformation of the incentives, motivations, and status of the workers, within industry ; (5) overall viability and capacity to meet crucial economic problems. It will be assumed, further, that Labour did not set out to achieve Socialism in six years, or, on the other hand, to develop merely *ad hoc* solutions, but, in general, to combine Socialist planning with control techniques that, in any event, would have been required.

Throughout, of course, it will be necessary to employ broad conceptual terms and characterisations, and here a word should be said about the way these terms are used. Wherever employed the term ' mixed economy ' refers to an economy characterised by (1) public and private enterprise, but with nationalisation confined to the basic public utilities and industries which occupy a crucial power position in the economy ; and (2) State regulation and control of the private industrial sector, particularly with regard to investment, prices, exports, imports, and other supply and demand factors. The term ' Welfare State ' is used to describe a mixed economy with an admixture of State responsibility for employment, social services, and an egalitarian distribution of income. ' Socialism ', in the present study, does not mean public ownership of all the means of production, or an absolute equality of incomes. Rather, the term refers to the existence of a public section of industry

' large enough to set the tone for the rest, leaving private industry to operate within a framework of public enterprise, rather than the other way round.'[1]

It includes the abolition of large concentrations of private capital, and unearned or inherited privilege. It refers, too, to consumers' and workers' participation in decision-making at all levels, economic and political. Finally, and decisively Socialism means the inculcation of a new social ethic, the origins of which go back at least 2,000 years : from each according to his ability, to each according to his need.

[1] G. D. H. Cole, *Socialist Economics* (London, 1950), p. 53.

CHAPTER II

PLANNING UNDER THE LABOUR GOVERNMENT

'Continuity of policy—even in fundamentals—can find no place in a Socialist programme. It is this complete severance with all traditional theories of government, this determination to seize power from the ruling class and transfer it to the people as a whole, that differentiates the present political struggle from all those that have gone before.'

SIR STAFFORD CRIPPS, 1933.

It is, of course, true that planning cannot be considered apart from the environment in which it operates, and British planning, by virtue of the fact that the economy is particularly sensitive to world fluctuations, was from the beginning shaped by outside factors. The first of these, in time and importance, was the war itself. The depletion of overseas investments and consequent reduction of their earning power; the loss of export markets and the conversion of industrial plant to war production; the running-down of industrial capital and trading stocks; and the diversion of manpower to military service were the conditions that determined the requirements of planning in 1945. Thus, the Labour Government, in addition to implementing the objectives of Labour Party policy, was faced with the prior necessity of carrying out an orderly demobilisation of manpower and resources, the re-equipment of British industry, and a substantial increase in export earning capacity. The continued independence and prosperity of Britain, it was clear, depended on her ability to pay her way in world trade, and toward this end Labour Government planning was largely directed. The social objectives of Labour planning were necessarily accorded second place. Through six years of office the attention of Ministers and their subordinates was focussed on crucial national and international problems; there was little time to experiment with new incentives in industry, new forms of public control, new methods of redistributing wealth. At the same time pressures on the Government, at home and abroad, favoured status-quo solutions. The perennial cry of the conservative forces, urging the Government ' not to rush their programme, and to place production and prosperity above party plans and policies ', threatening to meet ' with uncompromising hostility each and every proposal which could not be reconciled with our traditional views ',[1] created an atmosphere which stifled innovation.

But although the aftermath of the war made the planning task immeasurably more difficult, it also created certain advantages for the Labour Government. In the first place, the years of war-time planning made planning respectable. Since 1939–40 the British people had been conditioned to a regimen of planning and controls, and thus in 1945 the onset of a planning Government was neither novel nor unprecedented. For the most part, Labour Government measures did not depart sharply from established policies, and in the main they were generally accepted and honestly administered, in contrast to the planning experience in some other countries, notably France.

Secondly, as will be shown in detail, the machinery of planning that was used by the Labour Government was largely a war-time creation. Most of the controlling departments, agencies and committees had been established during the war, and were retained afterwards. Similarly the system of controls, or methods by which the controls were operated, originated, to a considerable extent, with the Coalition Government. As noted by the Permanent Secretary to the Treasury as late as 1950,

> ' The arrangements now used for the direction of our economic affairs are in part derived from the war-time techniques of programmes and allocations of resources.'[2]

It is also important that during the war the Civil Service had acquired some experience of control functions, and that the majority of war-time Civil Servants served, for at least some

---

[1] Sir Clive Baillieu, President of the Federation of British Industries, at the Annual General Meeting of the F.B.I., April 30, 1947.
[2] Sir Edward Bridges, *Treasury Control* (Stamp Memorial Lecture, London, 1950), p. 22.

period, under the Labour Government.[1] The continuity of experience, however, was not without its hazards. The conservative character of the Civil Service, a basis of selection which limited entry at the higher levels to upper class persons, remained substantially unchanged under the Labour Government,[2] and must have influenced the intellectual environment in which policy decisions were made.

Finally, the war experience had committed the Conservative Party to partial planning. The Coalition Government's *Employment Policy White Paper* of 1944[3] had accepted State responsibility for the provision of employment, planned investment, and the establishment of a planning staff to report on economic trends and developments. While the Conservative Party's conception of planning was certainly narrower than that of the Labour Government, there was sufficient common ground, particularly at leadership levels, to rule out resistance *à outrance* on the part of the Opposition. Differences between the Parties revolved around particular plans and methods rather than planning itself, although, of course, it was the function of propaganda on both sides to conceal any similarity of outlook. It was noted by R. A. Butler in 1947 that Conservatives

---

[1] The Civil Service, which had expanded to 184 per cent of its 1939 strength in 1943, did not fall below 174.5 per cent of the 1939 figure under Labour. Turnover in 1951 was estimated at between 25 and 35 per cent per annum for the temporary staff, $6\frac{1}{2}$ per cent per annum for the permanent grades. Letter to the writer from a Treasury official, October 22, 1951.

[2] It was noted in 1951 that 'War has altered the picture merely in inessentials, and a Victorian would be surprised only by the presence of women. He would be familiar with the social gradings of Civil Servants and would have difficulty in recognising a new century until he passed from Whitehall to Parliament Square. The widening gap between the social backgrounds and experience of Cabinet Ministers and senior officials emphasises and results from the rapidity of change in politics and the conservative pressure of professionalisation in administration. Open competitive examinations have all but limited entry into the administrative grade to those whose status has enabled them to pass from a narrow range of schools into the universities. . . . Just as the undermining of aristocratic England gave point and urgency to the reforms of the 'fifties, so now, whether we wish to recognise it or not, the passing of middle-class England raises analogous issues '. O. R. McGregor 'Civil Servants and the Civil Service : 1850–1950.' *Political Quarterly*, vol. 22, No. 2 (April–June, 1951), p. 162. It is also of interest that entry into the Foreign Service remained, according to *The Times* of April 17, 1950, 'much as it was before. Of the 250 successful candidates, 118 came from Oxford, 88 from Cambridge, 13 from London, 13 from no University . . . the deduction is that the Foreign Service is still regarded, however wrongly, as the preserve of the wealthy '.

[3] Cmd. 6527.

' are not frightened at the use of the State. A good Tory has never been in history afraid of the use of the State. The State is an agency, and the agency is subordinate to the needs of the individual. The State ought to be used in the interest of the people and the community generally. . . .'[1]

And during the 1951 General Election campaign, as the *Financial Times*[2] shrewdly commented,

' the issue of controls has hardly been mentioned . . . . Since controls are a subject of such warm dispute between the parties, it is surprising that neither of them, during the election campaign, has breathed a whisper about the Supplies and Services (Transitional Powers) Act (from which) most of the economic controls which affect the daily lives of every business man and private individual in the country emanate . . . .'[3]

Many Conservatives did not accept planning and the Welfare State, but the Party leadership, as was indicated by the appointment of R. A. Butler as Chancellor of the Exchequer in late 1951, had accepted as policy a high level of employment and welfare measures. Such an acceptance, in turn, meant that the Labour Government was able to put through Parliament the bulk of its legislative programme with a minimum of manœuvre and difficulty.

Thus, in a number of ways, the war and its after-effects both helped and hindered Labour Government planning and largely determined its direction. At the same time, post-war developments wholly or partly outside the Government's control had effects not unlike those which the war contributed. The sudden suspension of Lend-Lease in 1945, before the British were able to finance vital imports of food and raw materials, imposed a strain on the economy that was only partly relieved by the American and Canadian loans. The bitter winter of 1946–47, which reduced the food supply and sharply affected industrial production, was a

---

[1] From a speech in the House of Commons, March 10, 1947.
[2] All references to newspapers and journals are to British publications unless otherwise noted.
[3] *Financial Times*, October 18, 1951.

further worsening factor. Neither Marshall Aid, an increased volume of exports at the expense of home consumption, nor the devaluation of the pound in 1949, which cheapened exports, were able to solve the problem of a continuing trade deficit. Finally in 1950 Korea imposed a rearmament burden that the economy—and for that matter the Labour Government itself—was hardly able to absorb. While, initially, global stockpiling after Korea led to a substantial increase in the dollar earnings of the Sterling Area, 1951 closed with a soaring deficit on the U.K.'s external account and sharply rising prices at home.

Against this background, the Labour Government set out to achieve a number of social objectives, of which the most important were full employment and redistribution of income.[1] According to Sir Stafford Cripps, the goal of planning was

' to combine a free democracy with a planned economy . . . to create a Happy Country in which there is equality of opportunity and not too great a disparity of personal incomes. It is basic to that kind of life that there should be full employment and full participation by the workers in the industrial life of the community. How particular planning operations are carried out or how particular industries are organised is only important in so far as such matters are essential steps in attaining the goal at which we aim.'[2]

Democratic planning, however, was to be characterized by a minimum of compulsion and a maximum of ' agreement, persuasion, consultation and other free democratic methods '.[3] The definitive statement of the Labour Government's conception of planning, set forth in the *Economic Survey* for 1947,[4] pointed out that

---

[1] The overall programme of the Labour Government has been evaluated in a number of studies including the following : Bertrand de Jouvenel, *Problems of Socialist England* (London, 1949) ; Virginia Cowles, *No Cause for Alarm* (New York, 1949) ; Robert A. Brady, *Crisis in Britain* (Berkeley, 1950) ; Political and Economic Planning, *Government and Industry* (London, 1952). For Conservative critiques of the Labour Government see E. Devons, *Planning in Practice* (London, 1951) ; R. F. Harrod, *And So It Goes On* (London, 1951) ; John Jewkes, *Ordeal by Planning* (London, 1948) ; Ivor Thomas, *The Socialist Tragedy* (New York, 1951) ; and the numerous publications of the Conservative Party's Central Office.

[2] *Hansard*, Vol. 474, col. 39, April 18, 1950.

[3] loc. cit.   [4] Cmd. 7046.

' There is an essential difference between totalitarian and democratic planning. The former subordinates all individual desires and preferences to the demands of the State. For this purpose, it uses various methods of compulsion upon the individual which deprive him of the freedom of choice. Such methods may be necessary even in a democratic country during the extreme emergency of a great war. Thus the British people gave their war-time Government the power to direct labour. But in normal times, the people of a democratic country will not give their freedom of choice to their Government. A democratic Government must therefore conduct its economic planning in a manner which preserves the maximum possible freedom of choice to the individual citizen.'[1]

Further limitations on planning were Britain's ' special economic conditions ' ; a complex industrial system ; decisions dispersed among thousands of organisations and individuals ; and the public's habit of making purchases from a wide range of choice and quality of goods. Above all, it was noted,

' Our national existence depends upon imports, which means that the goods we export in return must compete with the rest of the world in price, quality and design, and that our industry must adapt itself rapidly to changes in world markets.'[2]

Planning, therefore, would be as flexible as possible :

' In our determination to avoid the waste of unemployment we must not destroy the essential flexibility of our economic life.'[3]

The system of planning, as described in the 1947 *Survey*, would combine

(i) An organisation with enough knowledge and reliable information to assess our national resources and to formulate the national needs.

(ii) A set of economic ' budgets ' which relate these needs to our resources, and which enable the Government to

[1] ibid., p. 5.   [2] loc. cit.   [3] loc. cit.

C

say what is the best use for the resources in the national interest.

(iii) A number of methods, the combined effect of which will enable the Government to influence the use of resources in the desired direction, without interfering with democratic freedoms.

The *Survey* itself was an attempt to recapitulate developments since the war ended, and to present plans and requirements for 1947. Thereafter, the *Surveys*, which were prepared in the first three months of each year, became an integral part of the planning system, although, as will be shown later, their concern with planning forecasts gradually diminished.

It was significant that the first *Survey*, setting forth in detail the Government's conception of planning, did not appear until early 1947. Up to that date the Government appeared to be largely content with its war-time inheritance. The apex of the planning system was then, and later, the Cabinet. Directly beneath it sat a number of Cabinet sub-committees, of which the Lord President's Committee, presided over by Mr. Herbert Morrison, held the main responsibility for economic affairs.

Assisting the Government and its committees were two expert bodies manned by professional economists and statisticians : the Economic Section, a major division of the Cabinet Office, whose tasks were to submit reports based on information supplied by the Government Departments, to forecast economic trends and developments, and to prepare analyses of economic problems ; and the Central Statistical Office, which was charged with the compilation and analysis of statistical data.

At the Civil Service level, four inter-departmental committees were established to consider programmes for manpower, materials, balance of payments, and capital investment. While the purpose of these committees was to apportion limited resources between various claimants, the task of a fifth Steering Committee was to ensure that the claims of the four official committees were kept within the total of available national resources.

This early planning machinery, it was clear, was primarily a system for rationing scarce resources. Allocations were made not to the requirements of a long-term plan but on an *ad hoc* basis according to immediate economic needs and to the influence of individual Ministers and Ministries. The Government possessed at the time no facilities for long-term planning, and had such plans existed no Minister was vested with authority to ensure that other departments would carry out the instructions of the plan. Contrasting the original planning machinery with what was later established, Mr. Morrison has written :

‘ In our first two years the main emphasis was on developing a system of co-ordination through Cabinet Committees rather than direct economic administration by one leading Economic Minister.’[1]

The need for more effective planning machinery was sharply underlined by the coal crisis of 1946–47, which caused a major, though temporary, disruption of the economy. It was generally accepted that the crisis could have been foreseen far earlier than it was and that remedial action could have been more quickly taken but for the excessive departmental autonomy of the Ministry of Fuel and Power.

After this the change-over from a ‘ system of co-ordination ’ to ‘ direct economic administration by one leading Minister ’ was slowly begun, although it was never in practice fully achieved. The first step was to attach to the Lord President's Office in 1947 a newly-formed Central Economic Planning Staff, consisting of higher Civil Servants and economists, under the direction of a Chief Planning Officer (Sir Edwin Plowden).

While its primary purpose was ‘ to develop a long-term plan for the use of the country's manpower and resources ’,[2] a secondary purpose was to strengthen the contacts of the Lord President's Office with the major Government Departments. It is important to note that the Central Economic Planning Staff was not analagous to a ‘ General Staff ’ for planning, as is sometimes assumed. The Prime Minister made it clear, when it was established, that all decisions on planning policy would continue to be made

‘ by the Cabinet and not by the Chief Planning Officer.

---

[1] Herbert Morrison, *Government and Parliament*, 1954.
[2] Statement of the Prime Minister, *Hansard*, March 27, 1947.

Responsibility for these decisions must, of course, reside wholly with Ministers.'[1]

Indeed, the ' General Staff ' idea was never popular in Government circles, chiefly on the grounds that it would reduce the authority of the Cabinet and Government Departments, and tend to shift responsibility to an ' expert ', non-political group which might or might not be sympathetic to the general programme. As Herbert Morrison put the Government's view in 1946 :

> ' Sometimes it is said—I think wrongly—that we need an economic general staff in the sense of a central body of economists and experts who would make the whole plan, get it approved, carry it through, administer it and execute it separately from the economic Departments of State. I think that is a mistaken conception. Such an organisation would become almost as big as the Government itself. The Departments of State which contribute to our economic affairs are very considerable in number. They spread over nearly the whole field of Government. It would not work, and there would be friction all round.'[2]

Having rejected the ' General Staff ' conception, the Government's problem, Morrison continued,

> ' was, and is, to bring about co-operation between the Economic Section, the Central Statistical Office, and the Cabinet Secretariat, and the appropriate officers, the experts, from the Departments of State concerned in these economic affairs, and then to build up from the economic Departments of State, together with these common service sections of the Central Government, an efficient economic machine on the official level.'[3]

A further change in the planning machinery took place in the autumn of 1947, influenced no doubt both by the convertibility crisis of the summer and by the Lord President's illness. Planning functions, together with the Planning Staff, were

[1] Statement of the Prime Minister, op. cit.

[2] *Hansard*, Vol. 419, Cols. 2130–2131, February 28, 1946.

[3] loc. cit. Morrison refused to say whether the Cabinet as a whole ' makes the executive decisions at the highest level '. Whatever the facts, he declared, ' the Cabinet as a whole must be responsible for everything that happens '.

transferred to a newly formed Ministry of Economic Affairs under Sir Stafford Cripps. Again the reluctance of the Labour Government to vest the Minister responsible for planning with real executive authority is apparent from the Prime Minister's statement in the House of Commons :

' With regard to the position of the Minister of Economic Affairs, his position is one of co-ordination. There is no question of interfering with the departmental responsibilities of Ministers. His function is, with the Chancellor of the Exchequer—and they act in closest co-operation—to co-ordinate the economic effort both at home and abroad in all its various ramifications.'[1]

Whether it is possible for two senior Ministers to simultaneously co-ordinate economic policy was—perhaps fortunately —never seriously put to the test, for in November, 1947, Dr. Dalton resigned as Chancellor following an indiscretion over the Budget, and Sir Stafford Cripps was appointed Chancellor of the Exchequer in his place. The Ministry of Economic Affairs was then abolished, but all its staff and functions accompanied Cripps to the Treasury. These events undoubtedly strengthened the planning system, since the responsible Minister now had a strong executive department from which to work. But ' co-ordination ' remained the keynote of Labour's planning policy, and the Chancellor of the Exchequer was never more than *primus inter pares*.

The third major change in the planning machinery affected the Ministerial Committees. Until 1947 the Lord President's Committee under Mr. Morrison, had been the economic policy-making body. Thereafter, the Economic Policy Committee became the most important Ministerial Committee, and in 1951 it consisted of the Prime Minister, Chancellor of the Exchequer, Foreign Secretary, Lord President of the Council, Lord Privy Seal, and such other Ministers as were from time to time summoned to attend. Subordinate to it but of substantial importance was the Production Committee, which dealt with industrial matters, and whose membership included the Chancellor of the

[1] *Hansard*, October 21, 1947.

Exchequer, President of the Board of Trade, and the Ministers of Supply, Fuel and Power, Agriculture, Transport, Works, Labour, and Health (by reason of responsibility for housing). To assist the Government in the formulation and execution of its plans, various advisory bodies were called into play. At the national level the most important advisory body was the National Production Advisory Council on Industry (N.P.A.C.I.) first organised in 1941 and reconstituted in 1945. Under the Labour Government the N.P.A.C.I. consisted of seven representatives of industry, nominated jointly by the Federation of British Industries and British Employers' Confederation ; seven nominees of the Trades Union Congress ; two representatives of nationalised industry ; senior Civil Servants from various Ministries, most frequently the Board of Trade and Ministry of Supply ;[1] and the Chairmen of the Regional Boards of Industry, which were the N.P.A.C.I. counterparts at regional levels. The Council, whose Chairman after 1947 was the Chancellor of the Exchequer,[2] functioned

' to advise Ministers upon industrial conditions and general production questions (excluding matters which are normally handled by the joint organisations of employers and trade unions in connection with wages and conditions of employment), and on such subjects as may arise from the proceedings of the Regional Boards for Industry.'[3]

Meeting normally every two months,[4] the Council acted as a clearing-house for discussion of questions of general interest to Government, industry and labour.

Labour matters excluded from the purview of the N.P.A.C.I. were properly the concern of the National Joint Advisory Council (N.J.A.C.), formed in 1939 and reconstituted in 1946. The N.J.A.C., composed of seventeen nominees of the B.E.C.

---

[1] Representatives of other Ministries attend when their presence is required.

[2] Sir Stafford Cripps was Chairman of the Council during his tenure at the Board of Trade. When he became Chancellor of the Exchequer in 1947 he continued as head of the Council, and the Council thereafter operated under the auspices of the Treasury.

[3] *Government and Industry*, H.M.S.O., 1948, p. 8.

[4] An Emergency Committee deals with urgent problems between Council meetings.

and seventeen from the T.U.C., together with representatives of the nationalised industries was established

> ' to advise on matters in which employers and workers have a common interest, and to provide for closer consultation between the Government and organised industry. It also provides a channel through which the Government can make available to both sides of industry confidential information concerning Government policy and the national economic position.'[1]

Meeting regularly four times a year, and more often when necessary,[2] its chairman was the Minister of Labour and National Service. As is evident from the above statement of its functions, the areas covered by the N.J.A.C. tended to overlap with those of the N.P.A.C.I. and it was occasionally suggested—although the suggestion was never adopted—that the two bodies be merged, or that an entirely new ' National Council for Industry ' be formed.[3]

Below the N.P.A.C.I. and N.J.A.C. were a number of regional and local boards and committees similarly organised to discuss and advise on economic questions at regional levels. The eleven Regional Boards for Industry, formed in the early part of the war and reconstituted since, consisted of an independent chairman and an equal number of industrial and trade union representatives together with the senior regional representatives of a number of Government departments.

Both the N.P.A.C.I. and the N.J.A.C. were war-time creations. To these the Labour Government added two further bodies— the Economic Planning Board, established in 1947, and the Dollar Export Board in 1949. The former body was composed of permanent secretaries of several Ministries together with representatives of the Federation of British Industries, the British Employers' Confederation, and the Trades Union Congress. Its duty was to advise the Economic Planning Staff, and the Chairman

---

[1] *Government and Industry*, p. 10.

[2] A Joint Consultative Committee functioned as the Executive Committee of the N.J.A.C., and met as often as was required.

[3] *The Times* on January 8, 1947, commented that ' There seems to be a strong case for linking these bodies much more closely or even for merging them into a real national council for industry.'

of the Board was in fact the Chief Planning Officer, Sir Edwin Plowden. The Dollar Exports Board, as its name suggests, was concerned with the promotion of dollar exports. Its membership consisted of a number of industry and trade union representatives, appointed as such, and persons serving in an individual capacity. Nominally an independent body, the Board[1] worked closely with the Government on questions of export policy, and represented industry in discussions with the Government of trade, raw material, price and exchange problems.

With the exception of the Dollar Exports Board, the planning machinery at the Cabinet, Civil Service, and industry levels was in fact completed by the end of 1947 and no important changes were made during the remaining years of the Labour Government. In the absence of major studies the exact relationship between the different parts of the machine remains a little obscure, but enough is known to depict the essential character of the British system of planning. As one observer has written, it would be wrong to say that

> ' Britain had an economic plan during the period if by economic plan is meant a set of economic objectives, integrated and consistent in their assumptions which the Government had decided to carry out and which they had the power to carry out.'[2]

It is clear from the 1947 *Economic Survey* that the Labour Government had early rejected the idea of integrated economic planning, and with it the idea of a strong Planning Ministry. While it was frequently argued that systematic planning was impossible in a country so much influenced by external circumstances, it is also apparent that the Government, for political and perhaps for administrative reasons, did not wish to carry out a policy of positive and detailed economic regulation which would have been necessary to reach stated planning goals.

The machinery itself suggests that—had shortages not existed—planning under the Labour Government would have

---

[1] For reasons which have never been made clear, the Board was dissolved in 1951 and replaced by an unofficial Dollar Exports Advisory Council.
[2] D. N. Chester. O.U.P., *The British Economy 1945-50.*

been largely confined to the compilation of economic information and of forecasts by the expert agencies—the Economic Section, the Central Statistical Office, and the Economic Planning Staff—with the use of a small number of key controls to guide resources into the right places. In other words, the shape of the economy, the decisions as to the quantity and kind of industrial output required would have been left substantially to market forces.

Given this planning concept, controls could be kept to the minimum, long-term planning could be largely dispensed with, and the Government freed from the burden of detailed economic regulation. It was towards this goal of essentially liberal planning that the Labour Government was moving throughout its period of office and with considerable speed between 1948 and 1950.

The acute shortages of the post-war period, however, necessitated much more Government intervention in the affairs of industry than the central planning machinery was designed to cope with. Close control over imports for balance of payments reasons and control over factory building because of an acute shortage of building labour and materials forced the Government to make detailed planning decisions and of necessity to attempt to integrate them into a consistent whole. But on what criteria should decisions be based? When, for example, building licences were granted, should the expansion of the motor-car industry be favoured over that of the aircraft industry, or should the chemical industry take precedence over both? If imports had to be cut, where should the cuts fall and what would their effects be? Clearly, if market forces are unable to operate, decisions of this kind can only make sense if related to an integrated and long-term plan for the economy.

In the absence of such a plan scarce resources were distributed, inevitably, among the many claimants according in the main to the skill and tenacity with which their points of view were pressed. In the end, of course, all important questions had to be decided by the higher Civil Service or Cabinet Committees who naturally took account of broad policy objectives. But their decisions, it is important to note, were often more the result of inter-departmental negotiation and amateur judgement than of consistent and scientific planning. The weakness of this method, as one critic has pointed out, is that

> ' The economic system is of such a nature that you cannot make sense of your interventions as a whole unless you give considerable weight and authority to some central Ministry or Department of economic affairs. The 'direction' of economic policy is, almost by definition, a central process; just as, for example, is driving a car : the feet, the hands, the eyes of an experienced driver act together, they are not co-ordinated by a Committee.'[1]

This then was the machinery, at the top level, with which the Government set out to achieve its economic objectives. The ' general idea ', Sir Stafford Cripps stated in 1946,

> ' is that we should use a number of controls in order to guide production into the necessary channels, according to the plan which we have formulated. The principal controls will be financial, including price control and taxation, materials control, building control, machinery and exports control. Those have been in operation during the war, and certainly, as long as there are scarcities to be distributed, those controls will serve to persuade production into the right and most useful lines.'[2]

Budget policy, which admittedly drew heavily from the teachings of Lord Keynes[3] was early described as

> ' The most important control . . . the most powerful instrument for influencing economic policy . . . which is available to the Government.'[4]

It was assumed that Budget policy would strongly influence the level of investment, public and private, and thus substantially determine the level of employment ; and further by roughly equalising the amounts of total savings and investment would remove the pressure within the country tending to drive prices

---

[1] Robin Marris : *Machinery of Economic Policy.* Fabian Research Series No. 168, 1954.
[2] *Hansard.* Vol. 419, col. 3211, February 28, 1946.
[3] The relationship is explored in P.E.P., *Government and Industry* (1952), pp. 11–18.
[4] Sir Stafford Cripps, *Hansard,* April 18, 1950.

up or down. The Budget, therefore, was directed towards achieving a full employment economy that did not generate inflationary wage and price pressures, and, at the same time, through full employment and tax policy, aimed at effecting a redistribution of income. A further aim of Budget policy was to keep in check personal consumption to free resources both for investment and for exports.

Although accepted as the main planning instrument the Budget was never expected of itself to maintain the required balance in the use of resources. Over investment, balance of payments and internal equilibrium, the three crucial areas of policy, Budget policy was reinforced by a variety of physical and financial controls.

Of the investment controls the most direct and the most successful was exercised over industrial building. Throughout the Labour Government's period of office no factory building or repair work in excess of £1,000 could be undertaken without a licence. While licences for small works and extensions were fairly readily granted, major projects were carefully vetted before approval was given. New factory building is not, of course, the only form of investment.[1] Other forms of investment, principally plant, machinery, stocks and vehicles were practically unrestricted. While building controls would themselves result in indirectly controlling much new plant, considerable quantities of plant and machinery were installed in existing premises and in the large number of redundant war production factories sold to industry after the war.

To supplement physical controls and to direct the flow of new capital, the Capital Issues Committee, a war-time body continued under the Labour Government, was empowered to approve or veto new issues on the capital market. Making its decisions in the light of occasional memoranda issued by the Chancellor of the Exchequer, the C.I.C.'s main contribution was to deny new funds to enterprises supplying inessential goods to the home market. Thus distribution, entertainment, insurance, hire-purchase and banking were rigorously excluded from the capital

---

[1] Between 1948 and 1950, buildings accounted for less than 25 per cent of total industrial investment.

market, while export-earning, import-saving and basic industries were accorded top priority.

Considerable difficulties, however, were experienced in judging the claims of the vast number of ' neutral ' industries that lay between the ' top ' and ' no ' priority groups. The C.I.C. was not equipped to make technical planning decisions and the Chancellor, reflecting the same weakness in the central planning machinery, was unable to give precise instructions as to the order of priorities to be observed. Nevertheless, between broad categories of industry the C.I.C. appears to have guided investment into the right channels as the following table[1] shows :

NEW CAPITAL INVESTMENT
PERCENTAGE RAISED BY GROUPS OF INDUSTRIES

	1938	1947–51
Priority	29.3	46.8
Neutral	49.0	46.8
De-priority	21.4	6.4

These figures cannot, however, be taken as an accurate reflection of the Government's success in steering investment, since the bulk of investment was financed through channels over which the C.I.C. had no control. In the first place the C.I.C. dealt only with capital issues above £50,000 ; those below—and many companies made annual capital issues of just under £50,000 —were free and there can be little doubt that the volume of capital raised below the level of control was substantial. Secondly, in the 1945–51 period, company savings were a main source of investment funds. Self-financing was deliberately encouraged by the Labour Government through official exhortations and through high discriminatory taxation on distributed profits. Between 1945 and 1951, for example, Imperial Chemical Industries spent £90[2] million on new capital investment, only £20 million of which was raised on the market. Of Unilever's capital requirements totalling some £192 million[3] no less than £131 million

[1] *Three Banks Review*, ' Social Priorities and the Flow of Capital ', by Edward Nevin, September, 1953.
[2] Imperial Chemical Industries, Ltd., *Annual Report for* 1951.
[3] Unilever, Ltd., *Annual Report and Statement of Accounts*, 1951.

was met from internal resources. While a detailed breakdown of the sources of new capital investment is not available, all the evidence points to the conclusion that internal savings were much the largest component.

The last major source of company finance was the Joint-Stock Banks which remained under private ownership. Official policy on lending reached the banks via the nationalised Bank of England which, like the Capital Issues Committee, received occasional—and generally identical—memoranda from the Chancellor of the Exchequer. The Chancellor's views, however, do not appear to have carried much weight. Contrary to policy, not only was the volume of bank advances extremely high,—and in 1951 this must be accounted an important factor in the balance of payments crisis,—but the attempt to shift resources in line with Government policy substantially failed. As the table[1] shows, the movement of resources between industry groups changed little compared with 1938, and not nearly as much as with the funds controlled by the C.I.C.

BANK ADVANCES

PERCENTAGE RAISED BY VARIOUS GROUPS

				1938	1947–51
Priority groups	..	..	..	19.6	24.8
Neutral groups	..	..	..	25.9	29.4
De-priority groups	..	..	..	54.4	45.8

Controls affecting the balance of payments were, in the short run, even more important than those over investment. The main threats to the stability of the Government and to its full employment programme stemmed from the difficulties experienced in financing essential imports. It was to be expected therefore that both the volume and source of imports would be closely watched by the Government. In 1951, after very considerable relaxations had taken place, Government Departments still imported directly about one half of total imports. The Ministry of Food, for example, bought directly 75 per cent of all imports of food and animal feed, and the Board of Trade and the Ministry

[1] *Three Banks Review*, September, 1953.

of Supply purchased 25 per cent of all raw materials. Raw cotton was bought by a public authority, the Raw Cotton Commission, and imported steel and scrap was purchased in bulk by the Iron and Steel Federation, acting as agents for the Ministry of Supply. Private account imports were regulated by the Board of Trade through a flexible licensing system which varied according to the severity of control required. Thus nearly all dollar and hard currency imports were strictly controlled by the issue of 'Specific' licences to accredited importers. These licences stated the value or quantity of goods which could be bought within a given period. Open Individual Licences were less stringent, generally permitting holders to import without restriction, but requiring monthly returns of all transactions to the Board of Trade. The least restrictive licence, the Open General Licence, which in 1951 was available for about 25 per cent of total imports, could be obtained on application and permitted unrestricted purchase from any territory for which a licence was valid. During most of the period Open General Licences were confined to Sterling Area countries, thus minimising the dangers of gold and dollar loss.

In 1950, however, Open General Licences were extended to Western Europe following upon a decision of the Organisation for European Economic Co-operation (O.E.E.C.)[1] to 'liberalise' trade between member countries. By the autumn of 1951, 90 per cent of Britain's imports from Western Europe on private account had been liberalised. This relaxation of trade barriers was accompanied by the establishment, in July, 1950, of a European Payments Union (E.P.U.) under which trade deficits beyond an agreed size were to be settled through gold payments by the debtor country.

These agreements turned out to be a serious source of weakness in the United Kingdom's control system. Stimulated by the new freedom, the value of Britain's imports from the O.E.E.C. countries increased from £575 million in 1950 to £923 million in 1951,[2] accounting for nearly a half of the massive

---

[1] O.E.E.C. consisted of 17 mainly West European Countries who were receiving Marshall Aid.
[2] *United Kingdom Balance of Payments White Paper*, Cmd. 9119, 1946–53.

trade deficit of that year and involving gold payments to the E.P.U. of $420 million between July 1951 and March 1952.[1] This particular drain on the reserves was only stopped by the wholesale revocation of Open General Licences by the Conservative Government in November, 1951, and in the Spring of 1952.

Control over imports, by licensing or Government bulk purchase, was joined by allocation of raw materials to ensure that imports, and home resources in short supply, were not wastefully distributed. Immediately after the war, the allocation system had affected a large number of commodities ; as supplies increased the list of controlled materials was gradually reduced until, by the end of 1950, it applied to a relatively small number of items, of which the most important were coal, soft-wood, sheet steel, tinplate and sulphur. Later, in 1951, the aftermath of the Korean war necessitated a large-scale re-imposition of allocation controls which were, in turn, abandoned as the supply position eased in 1952 and afterwards.

In contrast with imports, exports were almost completely free of direct State control. Having announced the target figure of a 75 per cent increase in the volume of exports above pre-war, the Government relied for success mainly upon its general financial policy and upon exhorting manufacturers to conquer foreign markets. Direct control over exports, for economic purposes, either through State trading or through a licensing system was, with minor exceptions, not attempted.[2]

To swell the flow of exports, general taxation policy, which was designed to discipline home consumption, was reinforced both by purchase tax and by physical controls. Clothes rationing, for example, which was not abolished until 1949 was maintained partly to ensure that increased textile production should find its way into export markets. In a few cases, notably decorated pottery, fine carpets, certain types of lace and silk net, home consumption was totally prohibited by statutory order.

[1] *Economic Survey for* 1952, Cmd. 8509.
[2] Goods of high strategic value required export licences throughout the period. The number of such goods was initially small, but grew considerably after the outbreak of the Korean war in 1950. These licences, however, were related to foreign, not economic, policy.

In some cases the Government related raw material allocations to export performance. From the end of 1947, for example, steel was allocated to the automobile industry on the basis that a stated percentage of vehicles would be exported, and until September, 1951, the silk and rayon industry was permitted to acquire raw silk only on condition that 50 per cent of the output was exported. In the case of Scotch whisky, which was an important dollar earner, through a ' gentleman's agreement ' with the Scotch Whisky Association, the quantity released for the home market was in fact regulated.

Although the ' dollar gap ' was a continuing source of danger to the British economy, the direction of exports was largely uncontrolled. Some schemes which combined incentives with persuasion were directly related to hard currency earnings. Biscuit and confectionery manufacturers, for example, were given extra allotments of fats and sugar for every ton of finished product sold in hard currency areas. Nylon manufacturers were expected to export 60 per cent of their hosiery production, with exports to hard currency markets counting double in the fulfilment of quotas.

But these schemes were exceptional and affected a very small part of dollar exports. Greater reliance was placed on the provision of facilities designed to encourage, rather than to force, the business man into the desired activity. Considerable financial assistance to exporters was provided by the Exporters Credits Guarantee Department of the Board of Trade. The E.C.G.D. was authorised to insure exporters up to a total of £600 million against a variety of contingencies including insolvency, or bad faith on the part of the buyer, war, cancellation of export licences by the Government, or any cause of loss outside the United Kingdom which was beyond the control of the exporter or buyer. Further, in 1947 the Government dispatched special trade advisers to various parts of the world and broadened the commercial sections of its embassies, legations and consulates, particularly in the United States and Canada. These advisers sent back a stream of information on the prospects and difficulties of foreign markets which was made available to British industry through Government Departments and through the official *Board of Trade Journal.*

These measures were not without success. Exports rose rapidly throughout the 1945-51 period and the original target of a 75 per cent increase over 1938 was reached and surpassed. Judged against the difficulties which had to be overcome, not least the strong pull of the buoyant home market, the achievement may well be considered great. Measured against Britain's need to establish a balance, and preferably a surplus in her overseas payments, the export drive fell just short of success.

This relatively favourable assessment relates to Britain's global balance of payments. The position with dollar trade was much less satisfactory. In spite of repeated exhortations and various kinds of assistance, dollar exports, as a percentage of total exports, rose from 11 per cent in 1946 to only 14 per cent in 1951. The difficulties of winning the American market should not be minimised. The United States administration continued to operate an obsolete tariff policy, quite unsuited to the new position of the U.S. as the world's largest creditor nation. Further, as *The Times* Washington correspondent noted in early 1950, the United States Treasury Department

> ' continued to behave as if imports were automatically undesirable and should be discouraged by every means in its power. The Bureau of Customs, which is one of its branches, never altered any of its intolerable procedures and, at times, even used them to cancel the effects of reductions in the rate of duty which had been negotiated by the State Department.'[1]

But, undoubtedly, a major factor militating against success was the reluctance on the part of British industrialists to exchange a protected trade position in the Sterling Area for the comparative insecurity of the dollar market. In December, 1949, after the Dollar Exports Board had been established and when the dollar export drive was in full swing, a Conference of the British Institute of Management heard of

> ' . . . the refusal of the industrialists present to " press on regardless " into the Battle of the Dollar Gap. So many speakers insisted that to divert exports from other areas which supplied us with our foods and raw materials would

[1]*The Times*, January 10, 1950.

D

fatally distort the British economy, that the resolution was amended to delete all mention of the dollar market and merely recommended group-selling to exporters everywhere. It is evident that if the Government wish to enlist the full co-operation of manufacturers in their Dollar Drive they will have to use stronger economic arguments than those of short-term expediency.'[1]

Export targets, and particularly dollar export targets, were viewed with apprehension in industrial circles. Although free to determine their own prices, manufacturers displayed a striking inability to adjust selling prices to market conditions. Prices appear to have been fixed, in the main, in relation to conventional profit margins and with little consciousness of national objectives. Thus, in 1948–49 when the American recession brought competitive selling conditions, tighter markets and pressure on the £, little attempt was made by British exporters to cut prices although their very large profits would certainly have permitted it. Again, in 1951, when import prices soared and world demand for manufactured goods was very high, the rise in British export prices lagged far behind. Industrialists themselves began to doubt ' whether this country is selling its indispensable export commodities dearly enough '.[2] Looking back on the events of 1951, it is fashionable in Labour circles to attribute much of the disaster of that year to ' adverse movements of the terms of trade '. While it is true that import prices rose very sharply, an important part of the resulting deficit could certainly have been avoided had export prices proved more flexible. In 1952 export prices caught up with import prices and the balance of payments was largely restored.

Exchange control was the last main control through which the Labour Government sought to bring its overseas accounts into balance. Beyond what was required to finance the purchase of essential imports, the use of foreign currencies held in London was strictly controlled. Tourist expenditure, for example, was never

---

[1] *B.I.M.* ' Reflections on Harrogate ', Management Bulletin, No. 6, December, 1949, p. 7.
[2] British Rayon and Silk Journal, June 1951, p. 95, Chairman of the Co-ordinating Committee of the Rayon Staple Spinners and Doublers Association.

1807522

allowed to exceed £100 per adult person, per year : and in several years the permitted sum was considerably less. Residents of the United Kingdom and other Sterling Area countries could not transfer capital into foreign currencies without the permission, —which was generally withheld—of the Bank of England. British citizens who held securities in foreign countries were required by law to sell their holdings for sterling.

There can be no doubt that these measures were necessary. The lack of confidence of the business community in the Labour Government, the high rates of tax imposed on industrial profits and large personal incomes and the precarious balance of the United Kingdom's trade, combined to make sterling an extremely unattractive currency to those who held it. To these factors must be added the large sterling debts, blocked in London, which were incurred by the British Government abroad during the war. Had sterling been convertible, as the ill-starred experiment of 1947 demonstrated, the United Kingdom's gold and dollar reserves would quickly have run out. Even for financing temporary deficits in current trade the reserves were dangerously small. Each autumn, when heavy seasonal payments for dollar goods had to be made, brought a noticeable weakening of the £. In September 1949, when the slight U.S. recession of that year had sharply reduced dollar earnings, the devaluation of the £ could not be avoided.

As the Labour Government discovered, both in 1949 and again in 1951, many loopholes in the exchange control machinery existed. When the £ was under pressure, currency speculation added to the Government's difficulties. Funds temporarily lodged in London were rapidly withdrawn, payment for sterling goods was postponed and repatriation of dollar earnings by British nationals delayed. Probably the largest single escape route for the flight of capital was through the far weaker exchange control systems of other Sterling Area countries. The movement of capital within the Sterling Area was neither controlled nor, as far as can be learnt, even watched. There was no obstacle, therefore, to the movement of funds out of London, and, once abroad, there were various means of translating sterling into gold or dollars. From the very nature of these transactions it is

impossible to give precise information as to the amounts involved.
The Labour Party itself has officially estimated that :

> ' of £645 million of private capital which left Britain during
> 1947–49 only £300 million represented genuine investment
> in new projects. Some £350 million was "hot" money
> quitting Britain because its owners disliked the Labour
> Government's policy of fair shares or were engaged in
> currency speculation.'[1]

Estimates made by the United Nations Economic Commission
for Europe[2] suggested that in both 1949 and 1951 speculative
movements were a major factor in the run on reserves. While no
attempt was made by the Labour Government to control the
movement of capital within the Sterling Area, it is significant
that in Opposition Labour has pledged itself to

> ' seek a Sterling Area agreement about restricting the move-
> ment of capital within the Area in case "hot" money again
> proves a menace.'[3]

Control over capital movements was not the only requirement
of Sterling Area planning which the post-war experience suggested. Another source of weakness was the lack of co-ordination
between the trade policies of Britain and those of other Commonwealth countries. Since the gold and dollar reserves of the whole
Sterling Area were held centrally in London, it followed that
heavy dollar expenditures by any of the member countries would
deplete reserves and weaken confidence in the £. Periodically,
Commonwealth Conferences were held to discuss general policy
questions, but these were infrequent and there was a noticeable
tendency for Conferences to take place after, rather than before,
a crisis had developed. In the whole of 1951 for example no meeting of the Commonwealth Finance Ministers took place. It was
not until January 1952, after the bulk of the gold and dollar

---

[1] *Challenge to Britain*, Labour Party Policy Statement, 1953, p. 6.
[2] E.C.E. Economic Survey of Europe in 1949, pp. 124–6 ; Economic Survey of
Europe in 1951, Chapter III. According to this source, in the second half of 1951
speculative activities may have accounted for a loss of $300 million.
[3] *Challenge to Britain*, p. 7.

losses had been sustained that the Commonwealth Ministers assembled and a common policy of retrenchment on dollar imports was agreed.

The co-ordination of import policies raises a major problem of inter-Commonwealth diplomacy, but as Labour now admits

'We cannot avoid a crisis under the present Sterling Area arrangements unless the other Commonwealth countries adopt similar methods. . . . It is clear that Commonwealth leaders should meet more regularly and frequently. Labour would favour a permanent Sterling Area Organisation on the lines, for example, of the O.E.E.C. But this could only work if all the members desired and accepted it.'[1]

It has already been noted that one of the major aims, and achievements, of Labour policy was the maintenance of full employment. In the post-war period, however, the problem was not how to maintain effective demand—the problem to which Keynes and Labour economists had in pre-war years addressed themselves—but how to control inflation. Full employment even in Communist countries appears to be associated with varying degrees of inflation. For the Labour Government, with its far less extensive apparatus of controls, the control of inflation presented a continuing challenge. A variety of techniques were employed to discourage excessive consumption. The undistributed profits of industry were taxed at a much lower rate than distributed profits. Personal savings were encouraged through a number of appeals and savings campaigns launched by the Government, and by an increase in the interest rate of National Savings Certificates. Consumption was restricted by taxation of income and purchase taxes levied on certain kinds of goods. Finally, rationing, food subsidies and price controls were direct attempts to maintain price and wage equilibrium.

These policies were, however, only partly successful. Severe discriminatory taxes on distributed profits did not prevent the continuing, though gradual, rise in dividend payments, nor did the Savings Campaign prevent a precipitous fall in personal

[1] *Challenge to Britain*, p. 5.

savings[1]—from £329 million in 1946 to minus £89 million in 1950–1.

Price control too did not function as effectively as it might and the cause of this must be, in part, attributed to the method of control itself. With the exception of the Utility schemes,[2] maximum control prices and margins were generally fixed in agreement with manufacturers at levels sufficient to guarantee a ' reasonable return ' to the high cost producer. Although this meant that efficient firms made lucrative profits, margins were never deliberately squeezed to the point where the inefficient had either to improve their methods or to quit their trade.

It would be wrong however to suggest that complete price stabilisation was ever possible for the Labour Government, or that lax price controls were the main cause of rising prices. During Labour's period of office, the prices of imported supplies moved steadily, and at times alarmingly, upwards. In 1951 import prices rose 33 per cent over the previous year. These movements lay outside the control of the British Government but their effects were inevitably serious since the value of Britain's imports accounts for nearly a third of the national income. The major internal cause of inflation was, however, the growing volume of wages, salaries and dividends over which the Labour Government never exercised direct control. It is indeed difficult to see how, in a full employment economy, inflation can be prevented without some kind of control, at the source, of personal incomes. In the absence of such controls the fact that uncontrolled inflation did not take place can be looked upon as one of the major achievements of Mr. Attlee's administration. For this much credit rightly belongs to the trade union leaders who exercised consistent moderation in presenting wage claims. Nevertheless, by 1948 wages and prices had chased each other far enough for the Government to issue its now famous *Statement on Personal Incomes, Costs and Prices*,[3] which urged restraint, except in very special

[1] National Savings Movement Figures, quoted by David Dear in *Personal Savings*, Conservative Political Centre, 1953. Figures for personal savings have to be treated with some caution since in official publications they appear as the residual item in National Income and Expenditure Accounts.

[2] The Utility schemes covered certain consumer goods, mainly clothing, textiles, shoes and furniture.

[3] Cmd. 7321.

circumstances, on both wage claims and dividend payments. This plea was not without success : between 1948 and 1950 the wage bill rose by only 10 per cent and dividends by only 2 per cent. But such a policy could never be more than a temporary expedient. In 1951, under the impact of rising prices, both wage and dividend restraint collapsed and the Labour Government was forced to prepare legislation, for largely ' psychological ' reasons, to limit dividend payments—in the hope that this measure would ease the mounting pressure for higher wages.

The price that the Labour Party paid for not controlling personal incomes is not to be measured by the cost-of-living index alone, important though the rise in prices was both politically and economically. Equally important was the strain imposed upon trade union leaders. It would be difficult to disagree with the view of one expert[1] on union affairs that

' Traditionally wage claims have been the main objective which monopolised the interest and energy of the active membership and this supplied the dynamic for trade union development. Restraint alone was bound to drive a wedge between the leadership and the rank and file or else to encourage that apathy which is the deadliest enemy of any democratic Movement.'

The Labour Government's view of manpower controls, as outlined in the *Economic Survey* of 1947, has already been quoted. Direction of labour which had been extensively used during the war, was specifically rejected as a control which distinguished totalitarian from democratic planning. Nevertheless, the exigencies of the post-war period forced the Government to retain some direct controls over manpower. In the most seriously undermanned industries, coal and agriculture, ' ring-fence ' arrangements were designed to prevent workers already employed from leaving. Under the Control of Engagements Order, 1947, men between the ages of 18 and 50 and women between 18 and 40 who refused jobs offered to them by the Employment Exchanges could be directed, as a last resort, to certain undermanned industries. These coercive powers which were disliked by both trade union and employers' organisations were, in fact, hardly

[1] ' Policy for Wages ' ; Alan Flanders, *Fabian Tract*, No. 281, July, 1950.

ever used and were finally revoked in March, 1950. Another less direct form of compulsion under the same Control of Engagements Order provided that workers could only be engaged through the Employment Exchanges. This enabled Ministry of Labour officials to advise or persuade applicants to apply for what, from the national point of view, were the most desirable jobs and at the same time to prevent the absorption of scarce labour in non-essential industries.

While a very considerable re-deployment of labour took place in the post-war period, the problem of how to maintain a satisfactory distribution of manpower in a full employment economy was among the most serious the Labour Government had to face. In some key industries, particularly coal-mining, the problem remained unsolved.

A national wages policy, by fixing wages in relation to manpower needs, would have given the Government far greater control over manpower distribution—and would at the same time have reduced inflationary pressures generated by wage increases. But to such a policy the trade unions were resolutely opposed : so much so that the T.U.C. would not agree to examine its possibilities.[1] Behind this refusal there lay strong and traditional trade union objections. The determination of wages has always formed the centre of trade union power and influence and the transfer of this central function to the State would inevitably have led to considerable diminution of union authority. In addition, the introduction of a wages policy would of course have upset traditional and closely guarded wage differentials.

But although a national wages policy was not in fact introduced, in certain industries union pressure and various forms of Government intervention combined to secure some remarkable changes in relative wage positions. Coal-miners, agricultural workers and dock labourers in particular, received wage increases far above the average for the period, and this certainly helped to

---

[1] At the 1951 Congress, the following resolution was heavily defeated : ' This Congress, recognising the inconsistency of supporting a planned economy on the one hand and of insisting on an unplanned wages sector on the other, calls on the General Council to examine the possibilities of formulating a planned wages policy and to place its findings before the 1952 Congress. . . .' *T.U.C. Report of the 83rd Annual Congress*, September, 1951.

ease chronic labour shortages. Nevertheless, with its reluctance to use coercion and its inability to operate a wages policy, the Labour Government was an easy target for the orthodox economists who argued that employment was 'over-full' and that a pool of unemployment was the only alternative method of attaining the required distribution of labour.

From this description of the planning machinery it will be clear that the Labour Government's apparatus of control was far from comprehensive. The ' unplanned areas ' of the economy including manpower, personal incomes, profits and exports were from the start large and important and constituted a major source of weakness to the Attlee Government. The ' controlled areas ' too, as the description of investment and import controls has shown, were far less tight and effective than was generally supposed. The general inference is not so much, however, that there were insufficient controls as that with better planning, more effective administration and better methods of control, more could have been achieved with the existing apparatus.

The Labour Government, however, seemed far more interested in removing controls than in improving or extending control techniques. As early as November, 1946, the Prime Minister had noted that

> We are not in favour of controls for their own sake . . . (but) while there are shortages there must be controls, in the interests not of sections of our people but of the whole nation. . . . As these shortages disappear so controls can be relaxed.

In 1948–50 when the economy appeared to be regaining both internal and external balance, there was a substantial shift away from planning in the direction of a free market system.

Physical controls, in particular, were considerably reduced. In November, 1948, there was the first of the so-called ' bonfires ' of controls which abolished a variety of restrictions that had formerly required the issue of approximately 200,000 licences and permits a year. Controls on more than sixty industrial commodities and a wide range of manufactured articles and household goods were discontinued or relaxed. The November, 1948, conflagration was followed by one in March, 1949, which removed the need for a further 930,000 licences and permits a year, and the quota system, which had limited firms in the volume or value of the goods they could produce, was almost entirely eliminated. 1950 was characterised by a continued decontrol process involving not only the extension of Open General Licences to Marshall Aid countries but also the relaxation of food rationing and price control, and the abolition of steel licensing (except sheet and tinplate), and petrol rationing. It was also in December, 1950, that the basic tourist travel allowance was raised from £50 to £100.

1950–51 was equally a period of departure from the original conceptions of planning technique. As has been noted, the *Economic Survey* for 1947, contained a detailed statement of Britain's economic difficulties, and a number of planning ' targets ' for the immediate future. The 1948 *Survey*, however, demonstrated that there was a considerable gap between estimate and achievement in certain areas such as manpower planning, and the scope of subsequent surveys was reduced. By contrast with previous *Surveys* the 1950 *Survey*, the *Economist* commented, was an

' humble document, meek almost to the point of being meaningless. There is nothing here of the notions of 'democratic economic planning' as proclaimed in earlier *Surveys*, which presented a working pattern for the year's economic effort and left all men of good will to work for it. Indeed, the perplexing thing about the *Survey* for 1950 is its lack of plan.'[1]

The 1951 *Survey* which, even more than the other *Surveys* was couched in the language of experts, discontinued a number of forecasts, and suggested that ' many of the quantitative statements' made were ' tentative and conditional '.

While 1951 led to a resumption of controls, it was clear that, for the most part, they proceeded from and related to difficulties that followed Korea. Had there been no Korean War, it is probable that Labour Government planning in 1951 would have been almost entirely confined to Budget policy and certain balance of payments controls. A substantial Labour victory at the polls in 1950 or 1951 would, of course, have resulted in an extension

[1] *Economist*, April, 1950.

of nationalisation, but the bulk of industry would still have remained under a private ownership and control less subject to Government direction than it had been in the earlier period.

In the retreat from planning several important factors were at work. First was the discovery of the enormous complexities and difficulties of State planning, both technical and political. During the formative period of 1946-7 when the content of the planning machinery was being decided, confidence was seriously shaken, first by the coal and later by the convertibility crises. Devaluation in 1949 and the balance of payments disaster of 1951 served to confirm the very serious misgivings which already existed among Ministers. Of great importance to Labour's future policy, trade union and political leaders outside the Cabinet became increasingly sceptical of the capacity of planners to provide solutions to fundamental economic problems. Confidence was certainly not enhanced by the air of surprise and the evidence of unpreparedness with which each successive crisis was greeted. Inevitably, a Government whose experience of short-term planning is unsuccessful and of long-term planning very nearly non-existent is not in a strong position to advocate planning solutions. No wonder too that Ministers were not reluctant to escape planning responsibilities and to revert to a substantially free market system as soon as opportunity arose. It was also an important consideration that when planning forecasts so often proved to be incorrect, the case for controls was difficult to sustain. If the gentlemen in Whitehall did not ' know best ', why, once chronic shortages had been overcome, continue controls, when at best there is a strong element of bureaucracy and rigidity in their operation? It is not surprising, therefore, that given the choice of controls without adequate planning or the flexibility of the market, even socialist academics should increasingly turn to the latter. No one can read the works of Professors Arthur Lewis and Meade[1] without recognising the force of their criticisms.

Secondly, there were great political resistances, arising from industrial organisations, to the maintenance let alone the extension

[1] W. Arthur Lewis *The Principles of Economic Planning* and J. E. Meade *Planning and the Price Mechanism.*

of State regulation. More will be said about this in a later chapter.[1] But reinforcing this consideration was the undoubted fact that the Labour Government grew increasingly aware of the difficulties of imposing effective controls on unwilling industries. As the 1947 *Economic Survey* pointed out :

' Controls cannot by themselves bring very rapid changes or make fine adjustments in the economic structure . . . . Indeed the task of directing by democratic methods an economic system as large and complex as our own is far beyond the power of any Governmental machine working by itself, no matter how efficient it may be. Events can be directed in the way that is desired by the national interest only if the Government, both sides of industry and the people accept the objectives and then work together to achieve the end.'

And later in the same document

' Under democracy, the execution of the economic plan must be much more a matter for co-operation between the Government, industry and the people than of rigid application by the State of controls and compulsions.'

The emphasis on the limitations of controls and the necessity for co-operation is significant. While it may in part be regarded as a recognition of the facts of economic life, or of the inherent difficulties of regulating a capitalist economy, it is also true that many Labour leaders, in particular Sir Stafford Cripps, were increasingly persuaded that the objectives of private industry harmonised rather than conflicted with the aims of the Labour Government. Given this conception, controls which inevitably cause ill will and friction with industry, are far less desirable than voluntary co-operation—and indeed if the argument is carried to its logical conclusion controls become scarcely necessary at all. A movement from control to quasi-control and ultimately to self-control by industry organisations can thus be safely undertaken. In the abandonment of controls these factors must be accorded an important place.

[1] See Chapter III, Controlling Industry.

But there are important opposing arguments that can also be advanced. Leaving aside, for the present, the validity of the assumption that private industry shared the Labour Government's objectives, could not the planning machinery itself have been vastly improved to remove its obvious defects? It is generally conceded that with regard to economic intelligence Britain's Labour Government was far worse served than President Truman's liberal administration. For example, the results of the first post-war Census of Production were not available until 1949 and the only Census of Distribution that has ever been taken had not been completed before the October, 1951, General Election. Input-output studies, essential to the making of intelligent planning decisions, were not available until 1952. One of the most important omissions, to quote Mr. Gaitskell, Labour's Chancellor of the Exchequer in 1950–51, was

' the really deplorable ignorance about stocks and works in progress. I have little doubt myself that our policy in 1950 and 1951 would have been more successful had we had accurate and up-to-date information on this point.'[1]

This was certainly a valid criticism : stocks had been run down to the danger point in 1950 and were then enormously increased in 1951, a major factor in the balance of payments crisis of that year. Further, balance of payments statistics were in some important respects misleading. Information available to the Labour Government in 1951 indicated that current trading accounted for a deficit of £521 million. Later figures reduced this to £414 million, the difference being largely made up by the increase in overseas investments, in which there was a large element of capital flight. Further, stocks and works in progress which were originally estimated at £315 million were, in later calculations, boosted to no less than £610 million[2]—an enormous figure which, incidentally, was only made possible by extensive bank credits. From this it is safe to conclude that important in- formation was not available to the Labour Government and that this seriously vitiated remedial action that might have been taken.

[1] *Fabian Journal*, No. 14, November, 1954.
[2] *Fabian Journal*, No. 11, 1931 and 1951, Thomas Balogh, December, 1953. Also Cmd. 8505 and Cmd. 8976.

The relatively slow reactions of the Labour Government to situations which patently required rapid correctives may also have been due to inadequate information. The tardiness in calling a Commonwealth Conference in 1951 has already been noted. But even more serious was the failure to reverse the policy of liberalising European trade. Open General Licences were still being granted as late as October 1951. In the judgement of the Economic Commission for Europe :

> ' More than any other the present crisis could have been foreseen and advance preparations made to deal with it. . . . There is little evidence however, that the authorities in either of the two countries particularly concerned—United Kingdom and the United States—had begun to adjust their thinking and policies to meet these difficulties.'[1]

The dangers clearly were not foreseen. Nothing else could explain the apparent complacency of Mr. Gaitskell's statement to the House of Commons in July, 1951, that the deterioration in the third quarter of the year was ' largely on account of seasonal influences ' and that

> ' so far as I can see at present the fourth quarter's results will not be so unfavourable, though again I think it unlikely they will show a surplus.'[2]

In fact, the gold and dollar reserves fell by not less than $934 million in the last three months of the year.

An explanation of the lack of economic intelligence can be found in the astonishingly small staffs employed in the planning agencies. According to one informed observer[3] there were never more than 15 people graded as economists in the Economic Section of the Cabinet and 15 graded as statisticians in the Central Statistical Office and many of these were engaged in other tasks, notably the preparation of routine publications and attendances at International Conferences. As far as the Economic Planning

---

[1] E.C.E. *Economic Survey in Europe*, 1951, p. 17.
[2] *Hansard*, July 26, 1951.
[3] *The British Economy*, 1945-50 : ' The Machinery of Government and Planning ', D. N. Chester, O.U.P.

Staff was concerned, between 25 and 35 persons were so employed. It is not surprising therefore that, aside from inadequate statistics,

‘No one ever found time for quiet reflection and serious forward-looking study. . . . There was an absolute rule in Whitehall that thought about the future is of minor importance compared with action about the present.’[1]

While the paucity of staffs and of information was an immediate cause of many of the difficulties of the period, it was certainly not the fundamental one. Lack of attention to the machinery of planning was itself symptomatic of the growing preference for a free market as opposed to a planned economy. Planning and controls were coming to be viewed more as necessary evils to be dispensed with as quickly as possible than as the indispensible machinery for Socialist policy.

To be precise, by 1950 the Labour Government was of the opinion that it had accomplished its immediate objective in the creation of a Welfare State. Full employment and taxation, it was argued, had produced a partial redistribution of income in favour of the working class; consumption generally had been characterised by ‘fair shares’; supplies and productivity had increased; industry had proved co-operative and, under Government stimulus, had become the enterprising and responsible partner of Government. Direct control, therefore, was seen to be much less necessary. The future role of the Government, it was believed, was to keep the gates of opportunity open to ordinary citizens, and to maintain, by indirect methods, the kind of economic environment in which opportunity could be realised.

The events of 1951, however, made it extremely difficult for the Labour Government to rest on its laurels. Apart from the economic crisis, the resignation of the three Labour Ministers in April, 1951, over rearmament policy marked the first major internal challenge to the Government, whose real significance, as subsequent events have demonstrated, is an attempt to move the Labour Party beyond the philosophy and conceptions of the Welfare State. At the same time, heartened by the swing away

[1] ‘ Machinery of Economic Policy,’ Robin Marris, *Fabian Research Series, No.* 168, 1954.

from Labour in the 1950 and 1951 General Elections, opposition-ist tendencies in industry and the Conservative Party were strengthened. Not merely in policy but in political technique as well, the challenge to Labour from this quarter was, is, and will remain, a formidable one. Hence, since 1951 Labour has been obliged to re-examine its assumptions and achievements, and, indeed, its whole experience in and out of power. To what extent policy has been revised in the light of the record is as yet far from clear. The only certain thing, as the following chapters attempt to demonstrate, is that searching examination of the achievement is required.

CHAPTER III

CONTROLLING INDUSTRY

' We have no room for controls operated by private industry and by trade associations.'

HAROLD WILSON, President of the Board of Trade in 1949.

' He who has in his hands the execution of measures is in very truth the master of them.'

SIR HENRY TAYLOR.

It is sometimes thought that the planning objectives set forth in Britain between 1945 and 1951 entirely originated with and were derived from the philosophy of the Labour Party. This belief, in turn, rests on the assumption that because regulations and controls are always characteristics of a Welfare State, something is planned and controlled necessarily for a Socialist purpose. In fact, as noted by E. H. Carr,[1] planning in the West has been associated primarily with the mobilisation of resources in times of war and other international crises. In recent history the vast extension of governmental activity has been a consequence, not so much of ' statism ', Socialism, or New Dealism, as of planning for war and quasi-war. The planning concept, in other words, connotes only an organised effort by Government to achieve certain ends. It tells us nothing about the ends themselves, whether good or bad, desirable or not.

The historical relationship between planning and war is particularly important in the case of Britain, and this is especially true with regard to the relations between Government and industry. The machinery of consultation, control and quasi-control, had been fully developed during the war, and with one possible exception (the creation of Development Councils) there were no alterations, or even major innovations under the Labour Government. The temptation, in 1945, to take over the existing system of relations between Government and industry can readily be understood ; certainly it was far easier to do so than to establish a new one. Nevertheless, the system operated by the war-

[1] E. H. Carr, *The New Society* (London, 1952), pp. 43-48.

time Coalition Government had been bitterly criticised inside and outside the Labour Party, and its continuance after 1945 must be regarded as one of the more puzzling and conspicuous features of Labour Government policy.

Both during and after the war liaison between the Government and industry was affected by a large number of boards, councils and committees organised nationally and in appropriate cases locally as well. While no fixed pattern of membership was adopted, the general intention was to create representative tripartite bodies which would include nominees of employers' associations, trade unions and the Government. The average industry-related committee thus included representatives of the F.B.I., the Association of British Chambers of Commerce and, rather less frequently, the National Union of Manufacturers ; a smaller number of trade unionists ; some civil servants ; university or other persons appointed in an expert capacity. Apart from the nationalised industries, which were compelled by Statute to establish Consumer Councils, consumer representation as such was less common than other kinds of interest group representation.

The most important of these bodies, the National Production Advisory Committee and the National Joint Advisory Committee, have already been described. But in addition a large number of industry-wide committees were set up to consider among other subjects science and technology, productivity, investment, and industrial research. While the number of these advisory and consultative bodies has never been formally tabulated, some indication of their range can be found in the fact that in 1947 the F.B.I. was directly represented on 37 such committees and councils and the British Employers' Confederation and the T.U.C. on an almost equal number.

In addition most industries and trades had their own separate advisory councils or committees, providing a further link between Government and industry. Tripartite in membership and usually consisting of nominees chosen by the appropriate Minister from lists supplied by industrial and union organisations, the advisory committees were constituted to discuss, report, and advise on matters of concern to the particular industry. Of the hundred or more such committees that advised the Labour Government, perhaps the most important were those in engineering, machine tools, vehicles, electrical plant, building, and shipbuilding.

Taking as typical one of these senior advisory committees for illustrative purposes, it will be seen that the Engineering Advisory Council consisted of twelve representatives each from industrial and labour organisations chosen by the Minister of Supply from nominations made by the organisations, and representatives of the Ministries concerned with the industry. Labour matters were dealt with by the Engineering Industry Advisory Panel established to advice the Minister of Labour on questions of employment. A number of smaller and more specialized committees in the industry supplemented the activities of the major bodies at both national and regional levels.

The frames of reference of the advisory committees were rather general, and usually stated only that a particular committee was established to provide a means of consultation between the industry and the Ministry. As may be expected, the term 'consultation' was given different interpretations by different committees, depending in part on the personalities and interests of committee members. In practice, the scope of the committees varied considerably from case to case. Some, purely advisory, were talking bodies rather than action bodies. Others were ineffectual either because they lacked authority in the industry concerned or because their functions were limited by the Ministry involved. A number of committees, however, were more than merely advisory or consultative. For example, the Engineering Advisory Council possessed quasi-executive powers. An official description of it in 1951 stressed that

> it is a very useful body which produces considerable dividends; for example, disseminating the doctrine of standardisation and the best techniques applied by the larger firms. It is a very powerful body, presided over by the Minister . . . follow-up action is taken. They do not just make a recommendation at one meeting and then forget it ; the important points are pursued.[1]

[1] Sir Archibald Rowlands, Permanent Secretary, Ministry of Supply, examined by the *Select Committee on Estimates* (*Sub-Committee* B), Tenth Report, Session 1950–51, p. 29.

An important contribution of the advisory committees was to provide forums of discussion in which Government, industry and labour could express their points of view, and, if necessary, argue and defend them. Through them the Government was apprised of prevailing opinion in an industry, and industry, for its part, was kept informed of changes in Government plans and objectives.

To the Labour Government, however, this elaborate network of consultation served the additional purposes of lubricating the machinery of state control and, in part, of replacing controls by voluntary agreements. The expansion of the steel industry and the establishment of the oil refining industry in the 1945–50 period were noteworthy examples of industrial development carried out by industry after consultation with the Government. Voluntary arrangements of this kind were, in fact, much favoured by Labour. ' Government Departments and Ministers ', a P.E.P. study[1] observed.

> ' believing that an ounce of willing co-operation was worth a ton of compulsion, set themselves out to establish friendly contacts and consultations and to use their compulsive powers as little as possible.'

In the actual operation of controls, however, major contact between Government and industry took the form of relations between a number of Ministries known as ' production ' or ' sponsoring ' departments, on the one hand, and individual firms and trade associations, on the other. Questions of import and export licenses, allocations of scarce resources, building permits, shortages of manpower and material—in short, the day-to-day requirements and problems of economic planning, were customarily dealt with by the Governmental and industrial units most directly concerned. While the top policy decisions were usually taken at Cabinet or inter-departmental levels, the administration of policy devolved on the production departments. It was these departments, in the main, where resided the responsibility for success or failure of the controls, that gave Labour Government planning its distinctive character.

[1] P.E.P. Broadsheet *Government and Industry*, Vol. XVII, No. 318, September 1950.

Thus, for example, to illustrate a major role of the production departments, 'global' allocation of scarce materials such as steel and other metals was made by the Materials Allocation Committee, presided over by the Economic Secretary to the Treasury and composed of representatives of the various consuming departments. In practice, the Committee would first determine the amount of material available over a certain period, and then divide the supply in accordance with estimates and requests between the consuming departments. The departments, in turn, determined the distribution between industries with which they were concerned, and even between firms within an industry. The basic priorities, in other words, were established at top levels, in relation to overall policy needs, but the effectiveness of the priority system and the whole complex of controls and regulations, was, in the last analysis, the responsibility of the production departments.

It would be incorrect, however, to regard the production departments as concerned only with detailed planning, or as related only to the Government. While the implementation of controls was their major function, they were charged with at least four other important tasks :

(1) to consider the place of their industries in the economy as a whole ;

(2) to sponsor the needs of their industries, primarily to assess claims for scarce resources and ensure that they were met, so far as was consistent with Government policy ;

(3) to expound and interpret Government policy to their industries, and equally to provide a channel through which industry views were communicated to the Government ;

(4) to collect and disseminate information about their industries.

Clearly, the production departments were the primary link between Government and industry, and it is to be noted that their working relations with industry were almost as close as their official relationship to the Government. With regard to industry, a P.E.P. study suggests, the production departments

> 'must have readily available information on the existing capacity of an industry, on the possibilities of changing it, and on present and possible markets at home and abroad. It will often be asked for advice by prospective new entrants or by firms wishing to expand. It must be able to give an answer which takes into account all the relevant circumstances of demand, prospects, supplies of services and labour, current policy on the location of industry, and the innumerable others which affect the final decision. It must be able to take up complaints and queries, answering them itself or seeing that they get to the right place. It must, so far as it is humanly possible, command the confidence of industry and do all it can to make the partnership of Government and industry a real one.'[1]

As might be expected, the importance of the production departments dates from the proliferation of war-time controls over industry. Before the war there were only one or two production departments, and their functions were rather limited. Between 1939 and 1949, however, the staffs of the industrial departments, excluding the Ministry of Works, increased almost ten-fold, from 14,700 to 113,300.[2] While the latter figure fell to 88,170 in early 1951, following the abrogation of a number of controls in 1949 and 1950, there remained eight principal production departments which, between them, were responsible for almost the entire range of British industry. The departments and their major industry responsibilities were as follows :

> *Board of Trade.* All industries not assigned to another Department, of which the most important were textiles, chemicals, rubber, and paper.
> *Ministry of Supply.* Iron and steel, non-ferrous metals, vehicles, engineering, explosives.
> *Ministry of Food.* Procurement, distribution and price control of essential foods and feed stuffs.

[1] P.E.P., *Government and Industry* (London, 1952), pp. 105-6.
[2] ibid. p. 98.

Ministry of Agriculture and Fisheries. **Farming,** horticulture, agricultural machinery, fisheries.

Ministry of Fuel and Power. Coal, gas, electricity, oil.

Ministry of Transport. Transport services other than civil aviation, road building, certain sections of the quarrying industry.

Ministry of Works. Building, civil engineering, building materials.

Admiralty. Shipbuilding and repairing.

In addition, the Ministry of Health, concerned with medical supplies and pharmaceuticals, was in some sense a production department, and indeed most other departments and agencies of the Government shared functions with or were consulted by the principal production departments from time to time.

The establishment in 1951 of a Ministry of Materials, in reference to the world shortage of that year, altered but did not change in essentials the machinery that has been described. The new Ministry was designed to concentrate responsibility for a large number of raw materials which had previously been the concern of various production departments, mainly the Board of Trade and Ministry of Supply.[1]

Although the Ministry of Materials acquired a number of functions formerly exercised by the Board of Trade, the Board of Trade remained the leading production department, and was, broadly speaking, responsible for all industries not assigned to other departments. At the same time, in its capacity as the most important economic Ministry after the Treasury, the Board of Trade was charged with general administration of insurance and company law, price policy and price controls, distribution of industry, commercial relations with other countries, bankruptcy, patents, census of production and distribution, enemy property and economic aspects of reparations, as well as the bulk of controls affecting production, raw materals, imports and exports.

While the Board of Trade in 1949 was not the largest industrial department, it was one of the largest, with a total staff of 12,694

---

[1] The Ministry of Materials was later to be abolished by the Conservative Government : its residual functions reverted to the Board of Trade and Ministry of Supply.

organised in nineteen major divisions. At the top administrative level, the President of the Board of Trade was assisted by two Parliamentary Secretaries, one of whom was responsible for overseas trade. Immediately below was the Permanent Secretary, aided by four Second Secretaries and a large staff of permanent civil servants. The Board itself comprised four principal departments : the Overseas Department, concerned with export promotion and licenses, trade treaties and agreements, and commercial relations with foreign countries ; the Home Department, devoted to general policy and control with regard to industry ; the Regulative Group, charged with insurance, bankruptcy, company law, patents, and administration of enemy property ; and the Common Services Group, consisting of the statistics, establishment, finance, and information divisions. In carrying out its tasks, the central headquarters was assisted by twelve regional offices which acted, in most cases, as the initial contacts between the Board and industry.

How did the machinery work? In the case of an industry under the general responsibility of the Board of Trade, an application for a permit or license, or merely a request for information, usually was first processed at the regional office level. If the matter was of relatively small concern it might be disposed of entirely at the regional level. Where, however, the application involved questions of major policy—location of industry, the allocation of scarce materials, building permits, export and import licenses— it was put in proper form by the regional office, often with a recommendation, and passed along to the appropriate section at the central headquarters, or to the particular agency or Ministry concerned. There the application might be disposed of, granted, or rejected. But if it involved a substantial issue such as, for example, large-scale investment or use of resources, it might await action by an interdepartmental committee, or even Cabinet decision. In practice, of course, most controls were effected at lower levels, and the average industrialist dealt primarily with his civil service counterparts. Where major policy was concerned, however, the machinery could and did accommodate exceptions.

It is important to note that the relations between controls and controlling agencies were rather complex, in some cases labyrinthine, and that they created some special problems for industry. The case history of an application for a building permit has been related by an informed observer, and can serve as illustration.

In the case of a proposed building costing more than £1,000 and over 5,000 sq. ft. in area, when the project has been formulated, the site chosen, and if necessary capital obtained from the Capital Issues Committee, the industrialist must obtain approval in principle from the regional controller of the department responsible for his production, assumed in this case to be the B.O.T. Application must then be made to the controller for a development certificate which will indicate that the scheme is consistent with overall U.K. location of industry policy. In major cases the application is referred to headquarters in London where there are two panels under the chairmanship of the B.O.T. representing all interested departments, or at the highest level, a Ministerial Committee on Distribution of Industry under the Chairmanship of the Economic Secretary to the Treasury. Next application for Town and Country Planning approval and assessment of development charges must be made to the local authority who deal with the local bye-law aspect and refer the application to the planning authority (usually the county council). At this stage local planning schemes, Ministry of Health standards for effluent disposal, etc., are considered. Application for assessment of development charges is referred to the Central Land Board. If all these hurdles have been successfully overcome, application must be made on the proper forms for building, sheet steel, timber, etc., and submitted to the regional office of the B.O.T. An application under £10,000 will be dealt with regionally and referred to the regional office of the Ministry of Works, Ministry of Labour and any other interested departments. If approved the Ministry of Works will issue the license and authorize acquisition of controlled materials. An application over £10,000 is referred by the region to the B.O.T. headquarters, where it is first considered by the 'production' department concerned. It goes next in the case of a small scheme to the Distribution of Industries

Department and may be approved by them and sent back to the region to be licensed, or, in the case of a larger scheme involving the use of much controlled material, the D.I. Department having approved it would refer it to the Ministry of Works to agree authorization of controlled materials. Ministry of Works cannot refuse the license but can defer the starting date. The application would then go back to the region for issue of the license. In the case of a major scheme, the Distribution of Industries Department would refer the application to an internal B.O.T. Committee under the chairmanship of the Second Secretary, before it went to the Ministry of Works.[1]

As may be guessed, it was popular in industry to charge bureaucratic excesses against the planning machinery described, and there can be little doubt that planning necessitated a formidable amount of paper work and form filling by industry. Between 1935 and 1948, according to the results of the 1948 Census of Production, the ratio of administrative, technical and clerical workers to production employees in industry increased from 13 to 17 out of every 100 employed,[2] and, in part, the increase was a consequence of adjustment to the control apparatus. At the same time, similar factors were at work in the growth of trade associations during the period. Most smaller firms, handicapped by staff shortages or uncertain how to proceed, turned increasingly to trade associations to represent them before Government departments[3] and in many cases, to handle or help with some of the paper work involved. While the larger firms also utilized trade associations, they were better equipped to deal directly with controlling agencies, either through their own special Government Relations Officers or, in at least one case, through

[1] D. S. Richards, head of the Government Relations Department of Courtaulds, Ltd., 'The Organisation of Management in Relation to the Requirements of Government.' Paper read before the B.I.M. Management Conference, October, 1950, pp. 6-7.
[2] *Board of Trade Journal*, January 9, 1954.
[3] Such representation became one of the most important functions of trade associations, and was marked by the frequency of advertisements such as the following : ' Influential national body, central council of a group of trade associations, requires Secretary to take full charge of its work, including committee structure, relations with Government departments . . . ' *Economist*, August 25, 1951, p. 484.

an entire, top-management related, Government Relations Department.[1]

Both the larger firms and trade associations enjoyed the further advantage of contacts with higher levels of the production departments. While industry was advised to make initial contact with the regional offices of the departments, the larger business units could, and habitually did, deal with the central headquarters, and usually with senior officials at the headquarters. As noted in the P.E.P. study,

> The standing of the big firm may be such that its directors can talk informally to, say, an Assistant Secretary or an even higher official, while the small firm has to be content with a Regional Office or with writing letters which are dealt with by Executive Officers ; there is thus a risk that the department will acquire a big-firm ' slant '.[2]

There was the risk that department officials would be improperly influenced by applicants, particularly when issues of major substance were concerned. Although the Committee on Intermediaries found the use of the ' 5 per-center ' infrequent in government-business relations, the bulk of applications, it discovered, was commonly dealt with by Executive and Clerical Officers of the Civil Service whose rank and salary were disproportionate to the character of their work and the amounts involved.[3] In the words of the Committee,

> Junior officials (often on low salary scales) habitually deal with, and in many cases decide, matters of great importance to the personal fortunes or amenities of applicants, and even when the decision is not in their hands their reports and recommendations have a considerable effect upon the fate of the application. There is an obvious risk (the extent of which we feel may not always be realised in the Departments themselves) that applicants may be tempted to try to influence the action of officials by improper means, and that officials may

---

[1] In late 1950 Courtaulds became the first firm to organise a special Government Relations Department.
[2] P.E.P., op. cit., p. 106.
[3] *Report of the Committee on Intermediaries.* Cmd. 7904, March, 1950.

succumb to or even try to initiate such proceedings, especially where there is a great disparity between the amount involved in an application and the remuneration of the officer dealing with it.[1]

The Committee found relatively few cases where improper pressure had been exerted. It did not fully explore, however, the significance for policy-making of social relations between Government and business officials—the luncheons and cocktail parties, the invitation to spend a week-end in the country, and so on.[2]

In fact, the available evidence suggests that, on the whole, the system functioned with a minimum of corruption.[3] It is tempting to account for this merely by invoking the tradition of morality in the public service and a high standard of ethics generally. But it is important to stress the nature of the controls themselves as an additional factor. Although the planning operation was often thought of, or at least discussed, as the chief concern of Ministers and the Civil Service it devolved in great part on industry itself, and especially the leading firms and trade associations. Indeed, the extent to which the Labour Government made use of business to plan and administer controls must be accounted one of its most remarkable and contradictory characteristics. Prior to 1945 the business-in-government features of successive Conservative Ministries had drawn forth bitter indictments from Labour Party members,[4] and major criticisms from House of Commons committees.[5] The system in all its

---

[1] ibid., p. 38.

[2] *E.g.* ' Coventry ' Group. Mr. W. D. Wilson, Chairman of the Group, reported that his Group intend to hold a Cocktail Party in November next, to entertain certain Government officials and others, and to give members an opportunity of meeting them socially.' *Engineering Industries Bulletin.* No. 85, November, 1950.

[3] An article titled ' Outwitting the Controls ' in the *Manchester Guardian*, March 4, 1948, reported that ' Pestering the controls is universally described as worthwhile. The impression is that actual graft is rare, but friendly personal relations produce favours.'

[4] See, for example, Ernest Davies, *National Capitalism* (London, 1939) ; Nicholas E. H. Davenport, *Vested Interests or Common Pool?* (London, 1943) ; Maurice Edelman, *Production for Victory Not Profit* (London, 1941). Davies served as Under-Secretary of State for Foreign Affairs in the Labour Government, and Edelman was a Labour M.P. 1945–51.

[5] Criticisms directed particularly at ' dual allegiance ' aspects of the system appeared in the successive reports of the Public Accounts Committees.

essentials, however, continued to function under the Labour Government, and while there were arguments for it, which will be considered, the retention of controllers drawn from industry must be considered a Labour Party concession of substantial significance. It was in fact true after the war, as it had been during it and before it, that in the words of the *Economist* in 1941

> Perhaps the largest reason for the growth in recent years, with the blessing of the State, of restrictive cartels and associations, is to be found in the unwillingness of the Civil Service to assume any responsibility for the conduct of business, even when that business is operating with the tacit or explicit sanction of the law behind it. The great defect of collectivism . . . is not that the bureaucrats will control industry ; it is that they will *not* control it but cede their duty to the private monopolists.[1]

In the early years of the Labour Government, particularly, the personnel of planning and controls was extensively drawn from the ranks of private industry. Beginning at the top strategic level of policy, the Chief Planning Officer, 1947–51, was Sir Edwin Plowden, a Director of British Aluminium and two other companies.[2] The Capital Issues Committee, whose position in the control of investment has been described, consisted of seven bankers, stockbrokers, and industrialists ;[3] the sole

[1] *Economist*, March 1, 1941, p. 264.

[2] Sir Edwin Plowden, although a war-time associate and close personal friend of Cripps, to whom he owed his appointment, was never associated with the Labour Party.

[3] In 1951 C.I.C. members and their principal business connections were as follows :

Lord Kennet, Chairman. Chairman Union Discount Co., Ltd. Chairman Imperial Bank of Iran. Director Equity and Law Life Assurance Society.

Sir Otto Niemeyer. Director Bank of England. Director Bank for International Settlements. National Bank of Egypt. International Nickel Co.

Sir Thomas Fraser. Formerly Director North British and Mercantile Insurance Co., Ltd. Formerly Director Finance Corporation for Industry, Ltd. Member Council of Foreign Bondholders.

Sir Percy Lister. Chairman and Managing Director. R. A. Lister and Co., Ltd. (engines, agricultural machinery, etc.). Chairman Blackstone and Co., Ltd. (diesel engines and agricultural implements). Director W. G. Armstrong Whitworth (engineers).

H. B. Turtle. Partner James Capel and Co. (stockbrokers). Member Stock Exchange Council.

(*continued on next page*)

Treasury representative on the Committee was the Secretary, and he took no active part in Committee deliberations. The principal industrial advisor to the Board of Trade for most of the period was the Chairman of the British Rayon Federation.[1] The majority of advisers and commodity directors of the Ministry of Food were unpaid representatives of business, in most cases of the leading firms in the controlled industries.[2] Indeed, the employees of one firm, Unilever, filled ninety posts in the Ministry of Food, twelve of them senior positions.[3] The important Steel Re-armament Panel of the Ministry of Supply was headed by a director of the Iron and Steel Federation, and the personnel of the various metals controls were largely drawn from the Non-Ferrous Metals Federation, itself a federation of trade associations.[4]

The leather controller at the Board of Trade until late 1951 was an official of the United Tanners' Federation.[5] The match controller in 1946 was an official of Bryant and May, Britain's largest producer of matches, and for a time had his offices on the firm's premises.[6] The paper controller was the Chairman of one of the largest paper manufacturing firms.[7] The footwear controller

M. J. Babington Smith. Director Bank of England. Deputy Chairman Glyn Mills and Co. (bankers).

M. F. Berry. Director Robert Fleming and Co. (bankers). Director Westminster Bank, Ltd. Director Standard Bank of South Africa, Ltd. Director London Life Association.

[1] Sir William Palmer.

[2] See Appendix I.

[3] Statement of the Minister of Food, *Hansard*, Vol. 435, Col. 15, March 17, 1947. In reply to questions which voiced objections to the presence within the Ministry of unpaid industry representatives, Government spokesmen usually took the position that, in the words of the Minister of Food on one occasion, ' it is not wise to swap horses in mid-stream.' See, for example, *Hansard*, Vol. 420, Col. 334, March 6, 1946.

[4] The Steel Re-armament Panel, although technically an advisory group, was ' rather more than advisory ; it does, in fact, take action, in consultation with the steel producers, to secure a better distribution of supplies of steel, particularly in the interests of re-armament. . . It has no statutory powers, but short of having statutory powers it is executive in that sense '. Testimony of Sir Eric Bowyer, Deputy Secretary, Ministry of Supply, *Tenth Report from the Select Committee on Estimates*, p. 61.

[5] Mr. G. R. White.

[6] When the Board of Trade was asked to arrange a transfer of the office elsewhere, a spokesman replied that no change was contemplated inasmuch as ' present arrangements have worked satisfactorily for six years.' *Hansard*, Vol. 424, Col. 191, June 26, 1946.

[7] Sir Ralph Reed, Chairman of Albert E. Reed and Co., Ltd.

was a director of the shoe manufacturing firm of Dolcis, and the hosiery, furniture, and tobacco controllers or advisors were trade officials.[1] Employees of Distillers, Ltd., occupied the top posts in the Molasses and Industrial Alcohol Control of the Board of Trade,[2] and the Cotton Control according to a Government spokesman, was ' largely recruited from Liverpool's cotton firms '.[3] The Board of Trade's largest control, through most of the period, the Timber Control, was almost entirely staffed by industry people, a number of whom, occupying senior positions, were unpaid.[4]

In addition to encouraging the formation of trade associations as ' umbrella '[5] or centralised ' policy-forming '[6] bodies in industry, the Labour Government often delegated to such associations the administration of controls. Thus, for example, newsprint was allocated by the Newsprint Rationing Committee, a trade body. Imported meat suitable for rationing was distributed by the Meat Importers' National Defence Association, Ltd., and the Wholesale Meat Supply Association, ' Government-sponsored associations comprising those firms which undertook the importation and wholesale distribution of meat before the war.'[7] The distribution of war-accumulated surplus stocks was undertaken

---

[1] Respectively, Major F. J. Stratton, C. R. Coleman, A. E. Walsh, and A. H. Maxwell.

[2] Reported by the President of the Board of Trade, *Hansard*, Vol. 436, Col. 28, April 17, 1947.

[3] According to a spokesman for the Board of Trade, in *ibid.*, Vol. 424, Col. 107, June 24, 1946.

[4] *Seventh Report from the Select Committee on Estimates*, Session 1950, p. viii. Of the nine controllers, deputy controllers, and senior assistant controllers, three were unpaid.

[5] Characteristically, an open letter to the Chancellor of the Exchequer in 1951, pleading for tax relief for wholesalers, began : ' I am instructed by the Council of this Organisation, which was set up at the suggestion of your predecessor for the purpose of providing an " umbrella " organisation to co-ordinate the views of wholesale distribution on matters of national and economic importance . . . .' The organisation, the Federation of Wholesale Organisations, has declared that ' its aim is to serve British Wholesalers in all industries in the same way as the F.B.I. serves manufacturers.' *British Rayon and and Silk Journal*, March, 1951, p. 75.

[6] Thus jewellers' associations which were reluctant to federate in 1946 were reminded by the president of one association that ' Sir Stafford Cripps has met representatives . . . to make it clear that we *must* either expand our Association . . . or, failing the achievement of this ideal, we must use every effort to federate in order to create one " policy-forming " body with whom the Board of Trade can talk business.' British Jewellers' Association, *Annual Report for* 1946, p. 8.

[7] Reported by the Minister of Food, *Hansard*, Vol. 467, Col. 60, July 19, 1949.

by Government-supported trade associations,[1] and during the period when clothing was rationed, the administration of the ' point ' rationing system was carried on by trade associations.[2] The cocoa and confectionery trade associations were largely responsible for a group of controls over the 'sweets' trade, and in 1950 they were given power to classify and distribute the relevant raw materials without further authority from the Ministry of Food.[3]

A number of controls were administered by firms, or a group especially organised for the purpose. For example, the Mond Nickel Company, on behalf of the Government, imported all nickel and allocated it to users through ' an unofficial allocation system working between the Mond Nickel Company and the Ministry of Supply '.[4] Sulphur for the manufacture of sulphuric acid was purchased by the National Sulphuric Acid Association, which consisted of three sulphuric acid producers.[5] When, in June, 1951, the Ministry of Materials became the sole importer of tungsten ores and concentrates, it was announced that the

> import and distribution of tungsten ores will be conducted through agents drawn from the trade, and for this purpose it is proposed to form a company whose management will include representatives of the following three firms. . . .[6]

Similarly, in the Ministry of Food and other departments, it was the policy of the Government to make the fullest use of the services of existing organisations. In the Ministry of Food particularly,

> Importers, brokers, wholesalers and others displaced by the Ministry's activities were . . . formed into associations to

[1] For example, the Government-sponsored Wool Industry Surplus Cloth Corporation was organised to buy surplus cloth, reprocess it if necessary, and re-sell it by allocation among members. It also advised the Government as to the best use for the cloth, whether utility or non-utility, for the home or export markets. *Board of Trade Journal*, September 29, 1945, p. 475.

[2] When the ' point ' system was changed in 1946, the reimbursement of traders for coupon losses was handled entirely by trade associations, except in Northern Ireland, for members and non-members alike. *Ibid.*, May 25, 1946, p. 656.

[3] Reported by the Cocoa, Chocolate and Confectionery Alliance, *Annual Report for 1950–51*, p. 5.

[4] Testimony of Sir Archibald Rowlands, Permanent Secretary, Ministry of Supply, *Tenth Report of the Select Committee on Estimates*, p. 32.

[5] *Hansard*, Vol. 484, Col. 2554, March 2, 1951.

[6] *Board of Trade Journal*, August 4, 1951, p. 228.

render expert services to the Ministry in the purchase, handling and distribution of foods as Ministry agents. The remuneration of these associations amounts to some £4 million a year and is fixed with the general intention of maintaining the earnings of their members at or about the pre-war level so that the trades will retain the means to resume their functions in due course . . .[1]

While the cost of the system was not the chief criticism against it, it was the subject of much adverse comment by the Committee of Public Accounts and other agencies. In the case of the Ministry of Food, the Committee noted that in a number of the trades receiving remuneration, some of the members did not work for the Ministry, others worked only part time, and some were engaged largely on clerical and routine duties. It was also noted in certain instances that the Ministry had been saddled with expenses that were difficult to justify. Thus £48,000 was paid annually to the oilseed processing industry for a number of closed plants that were not likely to be re-opened. Substantial amounts were paid to the Milk Marketing Board, under an agreement to compensate the Board for its administrative expenses and for the prices paid to milk producers, although the Board had accumulated a surplus by 1949 of over £2 million, and had refused to accept any change in the agreement that would reduce its income. The Ministry was also paying £2.4 million annually to sugar refiners, to compensate for the increase in costs since pre-war in the production of sugar for home consumption. It was noted, however, that information available for one large refining concern showed output and exports greater than in 1939, and that it was not until February, 1951, that the Ministry had begun an investigation of refining costs and profits.[2]

There can be little doubt, however, that in general the use of trade associations and bodies to perform certain tasks was relatively economical, and there can be equally little doubt that, for the most part, the businessmen appointed controllers and advisers by Labour were honest and able individuals. It was not on this

[1] *Trading Accounts and Balance Sheets*, 1950-1. Vol. 1. Report of the Comptroller and Auditor General thereon.
[2] loc. cit.

F

level, at any rate, that the system was most open to criticism. The essential question, rather, was whether businessmen, in the Government or through trade associations, are the best people to administer controls to which, in the main, they are opposed as businessmen.

Pressure to decontrol industry, put upon the Government by its advisers, was a factor of importance in the controls ' bonfire ' of 1948–50. It was an unusual week in 1951 when the newspapers and periodicals did not feature a detailed criticism of the Government policy by a present or former administrator of the policy. Thus bulk purchase of meat was attacked by the former controller of meat and livestock at the Ministry of Food,[1] and building controls by the former London Regional Director of the Ministry of Works.[2] Government milk policy was criticised by the Chairman of the Milk Marketing Board,[3] and the Chairman of the Cotton Board, while in that position, advised the Government that its

> attempts to intervene by regulation in the play of consumer demand, price, and quality are inconsistent with the situation in which our industry is called upon to export more than a quarter of its products to free commercial markets overseas.[4]

It is also of some interest that, on one occasion, a member of the Economic Planning Board, in flat defiance of top level policy, stated the need for a ' pool of unemployment '.[5] Controls, it is fair to say, are not likely to be best administered by hostile or antipathetic controllers; but aside from this, the effect of published criticism was to weaken public confidence, on which the control's ultimate success depended.

In the administration of controls, and in consideration of control policy, the advice of business-controllers inevitably reflected trade views and interests. The pressure for decontrol

[1] Sir Henry Turner, ' How to Get More Meat,' *Financial Times*, October 13, 1951.
[2] C. H. Kitchin, ' Simplify Building Controls,' ibid., December 13, 1951.
[3] Reported in *The Times*, June 16, 1951. The criticism was made while Chairman.
[4] Quoted in the *Manchester Guardian*, October 20, 1951.
[5] Questioned about this statement in the House of Commons, a Government spokesman replied that since the Board was an advisory body, the Government was not responsible for the views expressed by its members : *Hansard*, Vol. 443, Cols., 692–693, October 28, 1947.

has already been noted. Considerable care was also taken not to disturb the pre-war pattern of production and distribution in controlled trades. For example, the allocation of scarce raw materials was generally made on the basis of firms' pre-war output. While there were sound administrative reasons for this, there can be no doubt that this method of allocation, strongly favoured by business, was more in the interests of established bodies than in the interests of the community as a whole. In fact such a system of control, according to an Ex-President of the Board of Trade—

> perpetuates the pattern of a particular industry or trade, featherbeds the inefficient and unenterprising, freezes out the newcomers and penalises the efficient, growing firm. It has, in fact, many of the vices of the old, pre-war type of cartel, dividing out whole markets between producers on the basis of arbitrary quotas, and doing this with all the statutory sanction of the State behind it.[1]

It is significant too that no rationalisation schemes or long-term marketing policies were carried out although conditions were unusually favourable for their introduction. This is perhaps more a criticism of the Government than of its advisers since the latter could hardly be expected to formulate proposals flatly opposed to their interests as business men.[2]

A further objection to the Government's control system was that at the lower levels of administration the temporary status of control personnel greatly weakened their authority vis-a-vis the trades. At any moment the control staff might itself be disbanded and forced to return to private enterprise employment. In some cases the temporary status of controllers and their staff was further emphasized by arrangements whereby their salaries

---

[1] Harold Wilson, Ex-President of the Board of Trade, ' Private Enterprise,' *Future*, No. 1, January, 1954.

[2] The timber control provides an interesting example. Although there had been major changes in consumption since 1939, timber was allocated to merchants on the basis of their pre-war turnover. Thus Scotland, using more timber than in 1939, had to purchase it from quota holders in England, rather than acquire it direct from timber shippers trading at Scottish ports. The Timber Control agreed to change the system only if the change was unanimously approved by the trade. Lacking such approval no action was taken.

were paid, not by the Government, but by their ex-employers. In other cases, private firms made up the difference between Government pay and previous salaries. Advisers to the Government, even though they often possessed confidential information, were permitted to engage in business, and the members of at least one controlling-agency were ' permitted to keep in general contact with their firms, but not to engage actively in their day to day management '[1]

Sir Stafford Cripps did not draw a distinction between these two types of activity, and it may be doubted that there is a clear one. But surely devoted public servants were not likely to be gained by permitting businessmen to maintain ' general contact ' with their business connections and to continue on their pay-roll.

In the administration of price controls the influence of business interests on Government policy was a major fault. Apart from the utility schemes which were closely regulated by the Board of Trade, price levels were normally negotiated between the Central Price Regulation Committee, or its local offshoots, and trade representatives. Prices were too often established at levels set by trade associations whose figures for costs, profits, turnover, and other price components were generally accepted by the Committee. The resulting high prices were reflected in profits which were for most of the period the highest in the history of British industry. ' It is true that in the last six years ', a Conservative M.P. observed in 1951,

> ' since the war ended, it has been easier to make high profits without being really efficient than probably in any period in my lifetime.'[2]

An Oxford Institute of Statistics study in 1948 estimated that the general price level could then have been reduced by approximately 10 per cent.

> ' Defining fair profits for 1948 as a return on capital which has risen neither more nor less than average labour incomes

---

[1] e.g. Members of the Raw Materials Control according to Sir Stafford Cripps. *Hansard*. Volume 440. Col. 570. July 17, 1947.
[2] Angus Maude. *Hansard*. Vol. 493 ; Col. 248 ; November 7, 1951.

in private business since 1938 ; that is . . . as 185 per cent of 1938.'[1]

It was evident that in some trades, manufacturers never sold

' at less than the maximum prices fixed by the Board of Trade because the trade association concerned has forbidden it. This is a condition of membership of some associations.'[2]

In other cases statutory price control simply confirmed price levels already agreed by private price-fixing associations. Thus, according to the Proprietary Articles Trade Association,

' The arrangement between the Association and the Central Price Regulation Committee, whereby the latter recognises the Protected List as a list of " permitted prices ", continues to operate smoothly and to the convenience of the Association's members.'[3]

Whether or not it is true that prices ' cannot be fixed arbitrarily, since in the long run the control can only be operated with the consent and co-operation of the industry.'[4] it is difficult to avoid the conclusion that in many instances, the Labour Government's control system had the effect of giving Governmental authority to typical business practices and behaviour.

An alternative method of control, of course, would not have been, and never will be, easy in a mixed economy. It was a consequence of the war that a system of planning existed in 1945, and it seemed natural—certainly easy and convenient—to retain it in its essentials. It is also important that many Labour Ministers acquired their first experience of governing in the Coalition Government which made extensive use of business personnel, and, again, it seemed appropriate to carry on, if at all possible, with trained and experienced war-time associates. In addition, it was the cardinal belief of many Labour Ministers, that with the assumption of public office the businessman shed his identity

[1] T. Barna ' Those Frightfully High Profits,' *Oxford University Institute of Statistics Bulletin,* Volume XI, no. 7 and 8. (July to August, 1949), pp. 222-223.
[2] Eric M. Gammage, Chairman of W. Gammage, Ltd., ' Price Control Keeps Prices Up ' ; *Financial Times,* October 6, 1951.
[3] P.A.T.A. *Protected List and Year Book,* 1950.
[4] P.E.P. ' *Government and Industry* ', p. 80, 1952.

as such, and that business organisations charged with governmental functions in effect became, psychologically and otherwise, Civil Service bodies, with a correspondingly different set of principles and objectives. This belief, to some extent, reflects the public service tradition of the British ruling class, which has been one of its outstanding characteristics for several centuries. But it is also rooted in the common experience of Labour, Conservative, and business leaders, the shared background of public schools, universities, clubs, and careers which, in Britain, is a social link of major importance between persons of different political belief. There can be little doubt that this had an important bearing on the Labour Government's selection of key officials. Finally, it is probably true that in 1945 the trained personnel required could not have been found in sufficient numbers in the permanent Civil Service, or anywhere else but in industry.

The failure, however, to plan for the future is less understandable. Thus far, as will be shown in a later chapter, little has been done to train Civil Servants and trade unionists for industrial leadership, and if such education continues to be beyond the powers of the Labour Party, trade unions and the Co-operative Movement, industry alone will be able and willing to staff the key positions. Indeed, industry has not been slow to spell out the significance of self-government for the present and the future. Accepting the inevitability of some controls regardless of party or Government, one industry spokesman has indicated that the lesson is plain : 'We must learn how to control controls and make order out of orders.'[1] As for the role of trade associations, ' There were reasons,' reported a speaker to the Association of British Chambers of Commerce,

> which led him to believe that the Government would not be adverse to allowing industry to direct and administer its own controls, provided the Government were satisfied that the industries concerned were capable of doing it.[2]

[1] Paper read at the annual trade conference of the Wholesale Textile Association, quoted in the *British Rayon and Silk Journal*, May 1951, p. 48.
[2] Lt.-Col. Wentworth Schofield to the Annual Meeting of the Association of British Chambers of Commerce, *Report of Proceedings*, April 12 and 13, 1951, pp. 26–27.

A rather similar interpretation was suggested by an official of the Rayon Staple Spinners and Doublers Association. ' Our manner of handling the critical raw materials situation,' he notified members,

> has been praised by the authorities. . . . A very favourable impression has been created by our demonstration of what a properly organised industrial group can accomplish and this will in my view stand us in good stead when other problems such as defence needs and the ' Utility ' requirements have to be resolved.[1]

Whether or not these features of British planning can be reversed by a future Labour Government is a question which cannot be answered now. At present, however, an awareness of the personnel aspect of the control problem is not one of the outstanding features of current Labour Party policy discussion. As Balogh notes,

> There seems to be no realization that the spirit of legislation can be frustrated by the day-to-day approach and influence of the administrators, even if . . . they believe they are loyally carrying out the orders of the Government. . . .
> In the First War, Lloyd George tried to establish a system of excluding the vested interests from controlling themselves ; this example has not been followed. Since the inception of controls under Chamberlain a kind of self-government was established and this odd anomaly has not been changed since.[2]

It is to be noted, of course, that the problem does not admit of any facile solution. Nationalisation of key sectors of the economy does not necessarily imply, and did not in fact produce, a change in top managers and executives ; not does the present composition of the Civil Service suggest that it is wholly competent to exercise control functions. Much more could be done, however, in the direction of broadening recruitment into the Civil Service; in training persons drawn from the working class for positions of responsibility in State-managed industry ; in the

[1] Quoted in the *British Rayon and Silk Journal*, June, 1951, p. 94.
[2] T. Balogh, *Dollar Crisis : Causes and Cure* (1949).

development of methods for ensuring that policies and programmes are carried out, particularly at lower levels of administration. In all these areas very little was achieved by the Labour
Government. But unless the problem is faced, unless a way is
found to vote Socialists as well as Socialism into office, political
change, in Britain and elsewhere, will continue to lose much of
its significance.

CHAPTER IV

The Organisation of Private Industry

From an early date Labour leaders recognised that the system of controls inherited from the war would not be wholly adequate for peace-time needs. Many controls, as has already been indicated, were temporary in that their existence rested solely upon shortages of supply. As the supply problem eased, these controls were first relaxed and then abandoned. It was recognised too that war-time controls were directed more to preventing industrial action than to encouraging it. Looking ahead to a time when the domestic boom had subsided, or the world-wide sellers' market had dried up, this lack of positive power was seen to be an obstacle to the kind of measures which, in the interests of full employment and expansion, a Labour Government would wish to take. Even in the 1945–50 period, when controls were still extensively employed, the need was strongly felt for power to intervene more actively in business affairs. 'Private business', as one Labour policy statement[1] declared, 'is the nation's business'. Business had to become therefore efficient, enterprising, expansionist and co-operative.

These desiderata are easily stated but it was far more difficult, as Labour increasingly acknowledged, to work out the methods of achieving them. It should be noted that the Labour Movement as a whole, both its industrial and political wings, had traditionally given far less study to the private than to the anticipated public sector. For more than a generation nationalisation had been the focus of Labour's industrial policy, and debates at Party Conferences had been largely devoted to the selection of suitable industries and the working out of detailed plans for public ownership. The private sector, it was tacitly assumed, would rapidly wither away once Labour was voted into power.

This assumption was soon to be disproved. In spite of a hectic legislative programme carried out in extremely favourable

[1] *Challenge to Britain*, 1953.

parliamentary and political circumstances less than 20 per cent of the nation's productive capacity was successfully nationalised between 1945 and 1950. In the more relaxed atmosphere of the late 1940s another nationalisation programme of equal size, and carried out with equal speed, was hardly possible : and, in fact, Labour went to the polls in 1950 with a very modest programme which, had it been carried out, would have added at most 2–3 per cent of the nation's productive capacity to the public sector. It had to be acknowledged, even by the most ardent, that a mixed economy was inevitable and that the transition period would last for a considerable time. Private sector policy was, therefore, just as important as public sector policy and as the great bulk of export production was privately manufactured, in some respects even more so.

But beyond a rather crude anti-monopoly policy there were in 1945 few ideas and apparently little accumulated knowledge on which a private sector policy could be built. There was a tendency therefore in the absence of a more considered policy, to resort to the traditional expedients of subsidies and other forms of State aid to promote desired changes and improvements in industry. Agriculture was perhaps the main beneficiary. Direct subsidies totalled more than £24,300,000 in 1950–1,[1] quite apart from the guaranteed prices paid under the 1947 Agriculture Act. While substantial production increases were obtained as national policy required, farm incomes trebled in the 1938–51 period and there was evidence that the rewards for farming had reached a point where many farmers no longer had a financial incentive to raise production.

Other industries also benefited. The watch industry was permitted to lease Government-built plants for a period of 5 years at an annual rental of 4 per cent of the initial value, representing assistance of

> ' 75 per cent of the value of the plant provided . . . and somewhere between 5 and 10 per cent of the total cost of production.'[2]

[1] *Barclays Bank Review*, November, 1950.
[2] President of the Board of Trade, *Hansard*, Vol. 414. Col. 1045, October 15, 1945.

The film industry was aided by a loan of £6 million[1] and in late 1951 the Aluminium Company Ltd., was loaned the staggering sum of £40 million[2] towards its expansion programme in British Columbia. The cotton industry was given a re-equipment grant[3] equal to 25 per cent of the cost of new machinery or a total of £10 million in 1947–48, on condition that mills were grouped into ' manœuvreable units ' of over 500,000 spindles.

Under the Borrowing (Control and Guarantees) Act of 1946, loans up to £50 million in any one year could be made available to industry. In addition the Government supplied, through the Bank of England, one-third of the share capital in the Finance Corporation for Industry which provided funds for large scale industrial projects such as blast-furnaces and petro-chemical plants.

A number of research and promotional organisations were wholly or partly supported by the Government. These included in 1951 :

The British Standards Institution (£50,000).

The British Institute of Management (£55,000).

The Medical Research Council (£1,700,000).

The Agricultural Research and Advisory Council (£1,750,000).

The Council of Industrial Design (£268,000) ;

The Department of Industrial and Scientific Research (£3,000,000).

The Anglo-American Councils of Productivity which had, by 1951, sent more than 50 ' Productivity Teams ' to the United States to investigate and report back on American technology,

---

[1] Advanced to the National Film Finance Corporation which in turn made loans to film producers.

[2] *Financial Times*, 14 September, 1951.

[3] The Cotton Working Party had reported that only 26 firms, representing 20.4 per cent of the industry, comprised more than 200,000 spindles and only 5 firms more than 1,000,000. By June 18, 1947, 13 groups had qualified and applied for assistance *Hansard*, Vol. 439, Col. 34, June 24, 1947.

was partly financed by the Government[1] as were other organisations in the field of technology and invention.[2]

This listing of State aid to industry—and it is far from complete—indicates that the Labour Government made a substantial contribution to re-equipping certain sections of private industry. It reflected the awareness that, in the words of Aneurin Bevan :

> ' It is of no advantage at all to a Socialist that private enterprise should be languishing . . . so long as there is a private sector we want the principles of private enterprise to be as vigorous and revitalised as they possibly can be.'[3]

Useful as these financial aids were, they did not satisfy all Labour's requirements of the private sector. In Government circles it was felt that there was a need to create some new form of organisation through which desired changes in industry might be promoted and which would at the same time serve as a permanent means of communication between Government and industry. Out of these needs Labour's one distinctive policy for the private sector emerged : the Development Council. While these bodies owed much to the interest and personality of Sir Stafford Cripps, then President of the Board of Trade, their origin can be traced back to the strong pre-war sentiment in British industry—a sentiment shared, although for different reasons, by employers' organisations and by trade unions—in favour of rationalisation measures to remove excess capacity and to regulate competition in industry. In many industries trade associations had themselves succeeded in disciplining competition. But in others where, for various reasons, trade associations were weak the assistance of the State in establishing industry-wide regulatory bodies had been invoked. The most conspicuous examples of State intervention included the Coal Industry Act (1931), the Agriculture Marketing Acts and the Cotton Industry Reorganisa-

---

[1] The propaganda aspect of the Council's work expressed in a tendency to identify productivity with American-style free enterprise has been examined in John Cates. ' The Politics of Free Enterprise : Whose Productivity ? ' *New Statesman and Nation*, Dec. 29, 1951.

[2] For example, the National Research Development Corporation. It was established to exploit and develop, in the public interest, inventions which were not adequately used.

[3] From a speech to the 1949 (Blackpool) Labour Party Conference.

tion Act (1939). Many other industries affected by the slump, however, had pressed for similar measures and in 1945–7 the President of the Board of Trade appointed a number of Working Parties, 17 in all, to :

' Examine and enquire into the various schemes and suggestions put forward for improvements in organisation, production and distribution methods and processes in industry and to report as to the steps which should be taken in the national interest to strengthen the industry and to render it more stable and more capable of meeting competition in the home and foreign markets.'

Membership of the Working Parties comprised an equal number of industrialists, trade unionists and independent persons with one additional member as Chairman. Whether or not ' membership was representative, almost corporativist, rather than chosen for their special knowledge,' the reports did not propose, in general, sweeping changes in the structure and organisation in the industries concerned. There was general agreement that productivity, research and quality should be increased and that controls and taxes should be reduced. Prices and profits were found to be reasonable even where, as in the linoleum industry, there was a minimum-price-fixing agreement.

The most significant recommendation of many of the reports was concerned with the formation of one over-all policy body for the particular industry. Thus the boot and shoe, heavy clothing, light clothing, rubber-proof clothing, cotton, cutlery, furniture, hosiery, jewellery and silverware, jute, pottery and wool reports suggested the establishment of inclusive trade bodies or councils, either through the formation of new organisations or the amalgamation of existing ones. In some cases the establishment of Development Councils was specifically put forward.

Subsequently, in July 1947, the creation of Development Councils in industry generally was given Statutory approval in the Industrial Organisation and Development Act. The Act empowered the Government to establish Development Councils in any industry provided that such a Council was ' desired by a substantial number of the persons engaged in the industry '. It was made clear in debate that it was not the Government's intention to foist these Councils on unwilling industries although the Government's intentions, if faced with minority opposition, were not made clear.

Delegated to the Development Councils were a number of powers of which the most important was the right to impose a compulsory levy on those engaged in the industry, to keep a register of such firms and to collect statistics. In addition, Councils could undertake a range of activities designed to promote the general efficiency of the industry. This included scientific research, training of personnel, standardisation, improvement of design and quality and market research. Councils were also empowered to advise the Minister concerned on any matter affecting the industry. Where Development Councils were not thought to be necessary or, perhaps, where opposition was feared, the Act provided that more limited organisations could be established for particular purposes—for example for promoting research or exports.[1]

The Councils themselves, it is important to note, were to consist of equal numbers of representatives of employers and work people in the industry together with a small number of independent members, one of whom was to be Chairman. While the proportion of representative to independent members varied in practice from industry to industry (from 15 to 3 on the Furniture Development Council to 8 to 3 on the Cotton Board) the independents in all cases were heavily out numbered by the representative members. Since decisions taken by the Development Councils were governed by majority vote, independent members could exercise effective powers only in company with one or other of the two major blocs. In practice, however, as perhaps was inevitable, independent members tended to lose their identity and to become increasingly industry-minded.

---

[1] Thus the Drafts of the *Lace Industry* (*Scientific Research Levy*) *Order*, 1951, and the *Lace Furnishings Industry* (*Export Promotion Levy*) *Order*, 1951 provided that the levies raised should be used by the appropriate trade bodies for the purposes set forth. The latter Order, for example, imposed a levy of approximately £77,000 over a period of five and one-half years on persons engaged in the industry. The proceeds, the Order states, ' will be used by British Lace Furnishings (Overseas), Ltd., which is about to be established to finance the promotion of export trade in connection with the industry.'

The self-governing character of the Development Council is certainly its most striking feature. As noted in a P.E.P. study, the Working Parties and Development Councils expressed

' Two currents of thought—towards self-government on the employers' side and towards central control and workers' participation at the top level on the side of the unions.'[1]

While trade union support was a factor, it is still not easy to understand why such an organisation should have recommended itself to the Labour Government—nor the great efforts that were subsequently made to persuade industry to accept them. Even if enhanced efficiency was the sole objective of Government policy, these bodies could at best provide a number of common services for small firms to use or ignore as they pleased. The Councils were certainly not equipped to make radical changes in industry and, indeed, Government spokesmen were at pains to point out that their powers were mainly permissive and to reassure industry that they were not the thin end of the wedge of tighter control or public ownership. In the event, with the possible exception of the Cotton Board, the impact of the few Councils which were established was negligible.

While the debate on the Bill rather surprisingly failed to provoke any critical protests from the Socialist side of the House, it remained for a Conservative Member, David Eccles, in the very last stages of discussion ' to quote a few words from Adam Smith which seemed to be a salutary warning about this Bill '.

' People of the same trade seldom meet together, even for merriment and diversion, but the conversation ends in a conspiracy against the public, or in some contrivance to raise prices. It is impossible indeed to prevent such meetings, by any law which either could be executed, or would be consistent with liberty and justice. But though the law cannot hinder people of the same trade from sometimes assembling together, it ought to do nothing to facilitate such assemblies ; much less to render them necessary '.

[1] P.E.P. Development Councils, Vol. xvii No. 326. March 26, 1951.

I ask the House, Eccles continued,

> to consider seriously whether it is wise to adopt the principle
> that an industry ought to think as an industry. To do that is
> to be on the road to monopoly. There is only one industry
> in this country which thinks as an industry to-day, and that is
> iron and steel, and hon. Members in all parts of the House
> must ask themselves whether that is a good example.'[1]

At this point the debate was closed by a Government Whip.
The question which was barely stated was never answered.

The omission of criticism from the Labour side is even more
remarkable in view of the fact that when the Federation of British
Industries, a few months earlier, put forward rather similar proposals to those incorporated in the Industrial Organisation and
Development Act, the corporativist features of the proposals
were the subject of much discussion in the press. The F.B.I.,
following the publication of the first Working Party reports,
had suggested the formation of ' advisory or consultative
councils ', composed of industry and Trade Union representatives, with an independent chairman appointed by the Minister.
In the F.B.I. view, the Councils were to be advisory only ;
' The function of " promotion " should be vested in the Minister
whom it advises, and the implementation should be carried out
through the trade associations.' The F.B.I., however, was willing
to admit the necessity of statutory Boards in some cases, with
a composition similar to that of the advisory council, but recommended extreme caution in establishing such Boards.[2]

The F.B.I. report was greeted with some reserve generally,
and subjected to pointed criticisms, not merely from Labour
spokesmen but from industrial circles as well. ' But apart from
Trojan Horse considerations ', the *Financial Times* editorially
commented,

> ' The monopoly danger is implicit, even more strongly, in
> any organisation on these lines. It is precisely the industries
> and undertakings which operate under conditions most
> closely approaching monopoly which, in any case, can afford

[1] *Hansard*, Vol. 333 Col. 656, February 13, 1947.
[2] *Report of the Trade Organisation Committee of the F.B.I.*, October 21, 1946.

to make the largest concessions to their workers' point of view. They can most readily pass on any resulting cost increases to their consumers. The possibility of close sectional alliances between industrial managements and powerful Trade Unions, aimed at establishing something like an industrial closed shop against third parties, has always been present in many minds. Undoubtedly, considerable anxiety exists to-day lest, by the back or side door, something like the ' corporative system ', which flourished in some of the countries we fought against should gain a footing in this country.'[1]

The *Manchester Guardian*, in a somewhat similar comment, observed

' That we can have far too much industrial exclusiveness on both the employers' and trade union sides. If the relations between the State and industry are to grow closer the consumer must surely be allowed to have some slight influence. We do not want a corporate State.'[2]

Paradoxically, while the Industrial Development and Organisation Act marked an important advance towards industrial self-government, industry's attitude, after a short honeymoon period, turned increasingly hostile. So much so that despite the unanimous recommendation of 13 Working Parties on the need for an over-all body in the industries concerned, by the end of Labour's term of office only 7 Orders had been made under the Act. Of these, 4 had established Development Councils in the cotton, jewellery and silverware, furniture and clothing industries and 3 had authorised compulsory levies in the lace and wool industries. Although it attached great importance to the Act, the Labour Government was unable to reach agreement with the wool, boot and shoe, cutlery, pottery and china clay industries on the formation of Development Councils and in two cases conceded the point by accepting the creation of non-statutory advisory councils. Clearly the Government had suffered a major defeat on the whole issue of Development Councils—a defeat which was

[1] *Financial Times*, October 25, 1946.
[2] *Manchester Guardian*, October 21, 1946.

G

to be underlined by the abolition of the Clothing and Jewellery and Silverware Councils under Mr. Churchill's administration.[1] The reasons for industry's *volte face* on Development Councils deserve considerable attention. While political antipathies may well have played a part, an important reason was a change in the economic climate between 1945–6 when the Working Parties first met and 1947–8 when the Act began to be operated. In the earlier years it was widely feared that the post-war boom would be short-lived and that conditions of slump would again appear. In these circumstances Development Councils would have been welcomed as a means of avoiding chaos and price cutting in industry. It soon became apparent, however, that economic activity would continue at a high level for many years. Consequently there was little economic incentive to set up Development Councils after the Act was passed. Without this incentive there was no reason why industry should welcome an organisation which, in spite of its severely attentuated powers and corporativist character, might eventually serve as an instrument for state regulation and control.

But industry's main objection sprang from the fear that Development Councils would undercut the position of trade associations. Despite Government assurance ' that the Development Council will not in any sense supersede trade associations, any more than they will supersede trade unions ', it was the general opinion in industry that the potential significance of the Councils was as a replacement for trade associations, particularly in the relations between Government and industry.

Unwittingly, the Labour Government had, in sponsoring Development Councils run up against the most powerful force in British industry—one, moreover, which it had itself greatly strengthened.

By 1951, whether measured by number, size, or influence, the trade association had become the most representative form of industrial organisation.[2] There was also some evidence that they

---

[1] The Clothing Council was abolished in December, 1952, and the Jewellery and Silverware Council in February, 1953.

[2] The number of trade associations increased from an estimated 500 in 1919 to an estimated 2,500 in 1944. P.E.P. ' Trade Associations and Government ', *Planning*
(*continued on next page*)

had achieved a position of such dominance in industry that the Labour Government itself was unable or unwilling to challenge their authority in certain vital areas.

Paradoxically, however, both the long-term and recent development of trade associations owe much to Government policy and influence. Following World War I the Committee on Trusts (Shortt Committee) was able to state in its *Report*

' That the growth and powers of these Associations had been greatly strengthened during the period of the war, and that this result had come about primarily from the novel circumstances of the war, under which Government, acting through the Ministry of Munitions or other Departments, found it necessary sometimes to consult the most informed opinion of the trade, and sometimes to ration material through an organisation representative of the trade. Unassociated firms which found themselves not consulted by the Government were thus led to join existing associations, or in some cases to form representative groups for the purpose of advising the Government on matters affecting trade.'[1]

These precedents were extensively followed by the Coalition Government during World War II,[2] and, as has already been

No. 240, October 5, 1945. While there are no reliable figures for 1951, it is probable that there was a slight increase in numbers 1944–51, but a substantial increase in the size of trade associations, particularly the ' peak ' associations. See below pp. 91–2.

[1] Ministry of Reconstruction, *Report of Committee on Trusts* (Shortt Committee), Cmd. 9236, 1919. On the policies and practices of trade associations see particularly Board of Trade, *Report of Committee on Restraint of Trade* (Green *Committee*), 1931 ; A. S. J. Baster, *The Little Less* : *An Essay in the Political Economy of Restrictionism* (London, 1947) esp. chap. II, ' The Lunatic Years '; Robert A. Brady, *Business as a System of Power* (New York, 1943), esp. Chap. 5 ' Britain's " Feudalistic System of Cartel Controls " ', pp. 153–188 ; G. D. H. Cole, *British Trade and Industry* (London, 1932) ; Nicholas E. H. Davenport, *Vested Interests or Common Pool ?* (London, 1943) ; Keith Hutchison, *The Decline and Fall of British Capitalism* (New York, 1950) ; Hermann Levy, *Retail Trade Associations* : *A New Form of Monopolistic Organisation in Britain* (London, 1942), esp. Part VII, ' Present Trends and the Future ', pp. 221–253 ; and Part VI, ' Trade Associations and the Public Interest ', pp. 193–220 ; Arthur F. Lucas, *Industrial Reconstruction and the Control of Competition* (London, 1937).

[2] Aside from the effects of increased consultation between Government and industry occasioned by the war, the Coalition Government actively encouraged the formation of industry-wide organisations in various fields. At the beginning of the war, for example, in an effort to obtain foreign exchange an Export Council was established to form Export Groups in industry ; 280 such groups, largely coterminous with trade associations, were eventually formed, which firms were urged to join.

noted, were not modified in any important respect by the Labour Government after the war.

Thus a large number of trade associations list among their principal objectives the provision of ' a central body for the industry in its increasing contacts with the Government and Government Departments '[1] or the presentation of ' the views of the industry to Government Departments (thereby promoting) close liaison between these Departments and the various branches of the industry.'[2]   According to a P.E.P., study, ' pride of place ' among the declared objects of trade associations

> ' is often given to those objects which refer to the need of the trade in question to "speak with one voice" in negotiating with Government or Government Departments ; to promote helpful, and resist unfavourable, legislative and administrative developments ; to co-operate with Government ; and to act as a channel of communication between Government and the trade.'[3]

It should also be noted that many trade associations, together with monopolies and cartels in general,

> ' have usually been the product of depression and their policies a form of defence against such depression and its consequences.'[4]

In the years following the Great Depression a number of associations were established with the avowed purpose of regulating prices, reducing competition, allocating markets, limiting output, and generally stabilising trading conditions within an industry, and in some cases between industries. Under the Import Duties Act of 1932, industries were encouraged to consolidate in order to obtain tariff concessions from the Import Duties Advisory Committee established to administer the Act. Indeed, a number of trade associations, including the Iron and Steel Federation, were organised primarily to obtain such concessions. In practice,

[1] Association of British Chemical Manufacturers, *Report on the Chemical Industry*, 1949.
[2] British Plastics Federation, *The British Plastics Federation: Its History, Purpose and Function* (undated), p. 3.
[3] P.E.P. op. cit., pp. 2–3.
[4] J. H. Jones, *The Structure of Industry : A Study in Structure, Organisation and Control* (London, 1948), p. 129.

the I.D.A.C. was willing to grant tariff protection to organised industries which had not been able to achieve security through international cartel agreements.[1] At the same time, an application to the I.D.A.C. tended to strengthen the position of British manufacturers in negotiation with foreign competitors, and thereby indirectly encouraged the formulation of cartel agreements.[2]

By the end of World War II cartelization and restrictionism had become leading characteristics of trade association policy. The Federation of British Industries, the most important trade association, itself admitted, in 1944, that 'Assocations which aim at exercising some control over their industry' constituted one of two ' broad classes ' into which all associations could be divided.[3] It defined such control as consisting of :

   1.   Voluntary terminable arrangements for controlling prices, output and channels of distribution.

   2.   Arrangements which go beyond prices and output control and involve a re-organisation of the industry designed to control productive capacity.

   3.   The unification of selling activities under a central selling agency or cartel.

[1] Thus with respect to an application for a tariff increase from the Sheffield Cutlery Manufacturers' Association, the I.D.A.C. reported : ' We have received representations from the Sheffield Cutlery Manufacturers' Association that the present duty (on scissors) is inadequate to enable their members to reorganise their methods of production to meet the competition of the foreign mass-produced article either in this country or in the export markets. We think that there is adequate ground for increasing the present additional duty on the commoner type of scissors. . . . The application of the Cutlery Manufacturers' Association for additional duties also extended to other cutlery, with the exception of safety razors and blades. Owing, however, to an international agreement in regard to stainless steel, there is little foreign competition in this country in table cutlery. . . . We therefore make no recommendation in regard to this part of the application.' Quoted in P.E.P. op. cit., p. 6.
[2] An Annual Report of the British Chemical Manufacturers' Association stated that ' the Association has maintained its friendly relations with the I.D.A.C. Of the cases of applications for additional duties outstanding a year ago, the one in respect of celluloid has been withdrawn in view of an agreement between the British makers and their foreign competitors. . . . The case in respect of sodium chloride was withdrawn for a similar reason '. Quoted from *Chemical Trade Journal*, October 22, 1937, in P.E.P., op. cit., p. 6.
[3] The other class, according to the F.B.I., consisted of 'Associations which confine themselves to voicing the views of their members on matters of common interest '.

4. The unification and integration of the industry by outright combination.[1]

In regard to 1. the F.B.I. held that

'Branches of industry where circumstances make it desirable that some control should be exercised over production and/or prices occupy a special position. This form of control is handled in special ways. It is commonly confined to one or more sections only of the field covered by the representative association for the trade, and is usually exercised by private arrangements between the firms concerned, or through special sectional associations or companies formed for the purpose. It is not customarily dealt with by the general 'representational' association for the industry.'[2]

While it is probably true that the bulk of trade associations do not themselves control production and/or prices, it is equally true that most associations exist, in whole or in part, to facilitate such control by members. Thus, for example, the Federation of British Rubber and Allied Manufacturers' Associations does not itself deal with prices, but 'most of the twenty-four different production associations in the industry do regulate prices in an informal way'.[3] Through a mutuality of interest, which it is one of the functions of trade associations to create, effective if informal control can be and is achieved in most cases. As put by the Director of the British Electrical and Allied Manufacturers' Association,

'by its constitution, the Association is debarred from undertaking anything in the nature of compulsory price control. Nevertheless, it will be easily understood that with so many firms having similar interests, and coming into association through B.E.A.M.A., mutual arrangements between members

[1] F.B.I. *The Organisation of British Industry* : *Report of the F.B.I. Organisation of Industry Committee* (October, 1944), p. 19.
[2] ibid., p. 10. It is rather interesting that one member of the Committee, Laurence J. Cadbury, 'signed the report subject to reservation . . . that he does not regard it desirable for general 'representational' associations under normal conditions to control selling prices,' p. 14.
[3] P.E.P., 'British Trade Association,' *Planning No.* 221, May 12, 1944, pp. 15-16.

might be entered into by which competition could be tempered by co-operation, the disastrous price-cutting which was stagnating the industry in pre-war years could be eliminated and workable methods evolved by which reasonable prices should be charged for the more standardised classes of manufacturers.'[1]

Although ' mutual arrangements' between association members is probably the chief device of control, it is worth noting that a substantial number of trade associations, particularly in manufacturing and retailing, directly enforce regulations. The Proprietary Articles Trade Association, for example, which is primarily concerned with the drug trade, has among its declared objects

' The taking of such steps as the Association may be advised are legal to deal with extreme cutting of prices . . .'[2]

Moreover, a former president of a leading trade association has stated that

' the rules of nine out of eleven associations which he happened to have examined included price regulation among the objects . . .'[3]

Contrary to the F.B.I.'s finding, agreements restricting prices, output, and channels of distribution are not always ' voluntary ' or ' terminable '. A number of associations restrict membership,[4]

---

[1] Quoted from the *Electrical Review*, January 27, 1939, in P.E.P., ibid., p. 16.

[2] P.A.T.A., *Protected List and Year Book*, 1950–51, p. 11. The P.A.T.A., whose membership in 1951 consisted of 412 manufacturers, 60 wholesalers, and 10,750 retailers, has declared that ' the main object of the Association has been the elimination or control of price cutting ' with reference to ' any proprietary or branded article dealt in or proposed to be dealt in by the drug trade '. Pursuant to this object it operates a ' stop list ' of firms who have violated price agreements ; and in 1950 it investigated 1,700 allegations of such violations. ibid., pp. 11.14. According to *The Director* for July, 1951, legal counsel to the P.A.T.A. at the time it drew up its rules was Sir Stafford Cripps !

[3] Mr. L. V. Kenward, former President of the British Rubber and Allied Manufacturers' Associations, quoted in P.E.P., ' British Trade Associations ', op. cit., p. 14.

[4] Defining the qualifications for membership, by specifying minimum turnover, sales, staff, inventory, or simply stating that the applicant be a *bona fide* manufacturer or trader, with the interpretation of *bona fide* left to the Association, constitutes one of the most effective devices utilised by trade associations to restrict competition. On this point see Hermann Levy, ' Control of Qualifications ', In *Retail Trade Associations*, Chap. 16, pp. 173–191.

and prohibit members from trading with non-members. In some cases, violations of Association rules may lead to expulsion, with consequent loss of business, and in at least one known case, payment of fines totalling as much as £1,000.[1] While membership in trade associations is not technically obligatory, the operation of preferential rebate and exclusive dealing arrangements for members has the effect of making such membership a practical necessity.[2] Conversely, the establishment of a favoured position for firms in an industry, and of advantageous trading policies for the industry as a whole, constitutes a principal objective of trade associations.

A third factor in the formation of trade associations has been the desire by industry for a considerable measure of self-government, and an awareness that, failing successful self-regulation, the State would enlarge its area of control. ' If industry is to be relieved of bureaucratic control in the post-war period ', a leading industrialist stated in 1945,

> it must be able to assume the responsibility of governing itself in the national interest and making such contribution to national well-being as will ensure the full employment policy which the Government has promised. Any failure to accomplish this must compel the Government of the day to attempt to achieve full employment by the direction and regulation of industry under some system of controls. . . . Thus the organisation of trades and industries in associations is an essential factor if an effective post-war national policy is to be realised in time to prevent an unemployment problem arising on a scale unprecedented in history. Such trade associations must secure the loyal adherence of their constituent members and their agreement to conform to the

[1] Rule Eleven, Association of Dental Manufacturers and Trades of the United Kingdom. The rules of the Association were revised following an investigation by the Monopolies Commission in 1951.

[2] Thus, in one case known to the writer, a distributor of laboratory ware, who had been engaged in the business for fifteen years, was unable after the war to join the appropriate trade association, and therefore unable to secure the 15 per cent rebate granted to distributor members of the association. As a consequence, he was forced to stop dealing in laboratory ware.

policy devised by any Council or Executive Committee they may appoint for the purpose.[1]

By 1951 there was general agreement in business circles that organisation in and regulation through trade associations had been a success. Once again it was stressed that ' voluntary means of regulating our trade in connection with some of the immediate problems ' were preferable to direction by Government. ' Much can be done ' said the Chairman of Fine Spinners and Doublers, Ltd., in August, 1951,

> by voluntary arrangements to avoid the more unpleasant alternatives which could have a most depressing and stultifying effect on our progress. It would be a great pity if organised methods of self-regulation failed after they have succeeded so well since the end of the war.[2]

While self-regulation through the medium of the trade association was occasionally criticised by industrialists, chiefly on the score that it had been carried too far,[3] to the vast bulk of British businessmen self-regulation had proved a desirable and effective alternative to what was often termed 'bureaucratic control'. There can be little doubt that the successful practice of self-regulation by trade associations was in large measure responsible for their growth in size and influence during the period.

In turn, the acceptance of self-regulation by trade associations and industry generally owed much to the influence and authority of the Federation of British Industries, and its employer counterpart, the British Employers Confederation. Both had long maintained that, in the words of the President of the F.B.I. in 1948 :

> A frontal attack on controls will not be successful, but if we can prove that Industry is sufficiently responsibly-minded to

[1] Sir William Larke, Past President of the National Council of Building Material Producers, in the *F.B.I. Journal*, quoted in National Council of Building Materials Producers, *Memorandum on the Report of the Ministry of Works Committee of Enquiry on the Distribution of Building Materials and Components*, May, 1948, p. 6.

[2] Annual General Meeting, reported in the *Financial Times*, August 1, 1951.

[3] e.g. Viscount Hinchingbrooke, an industrialist and Conservative M.P,. in the House of Commons. :

' I have felt for some time now that there are signs of danger even in the voluntary formation of trade organisations in industry. In electricity supplies, telephone cables, and so on, the indications are that too much of a monopoly is being created by voluntary effort.' *Hansard*, Vol. 469, col. 336, November 1, 1949.

be trusted to control itself within broad limits laid down by the Government, we may be able to shift the basis from detailed Governmental control to internal industrial administration, and that is the most promising method of tackling the problem. . . . While, so far, our industrial organisation has proved equal to these tasks, and I feel very grateful for the hard work and loyalty that has been widely shown, I must confess to some misgivings about the future. I have misgivings in regard to the trend of Government policy, and I have misgivings in regard to the adequacy in some directions of our Trade Associations to assume the heavy responsibilities entailed in carrying out, by voluntary means, various of the activities and controls at present operated by Government. Taking this second point first, I know the sacrifices that have been made by the leaders in many industries to further the work of their Trade Organisations. I appreciate only too well the heavy burden of worry and labour borne by the officials of Trade Associations and the sacrifices which the members of these Associations have made in order to conform with wider interests. But unless we can develop further Industry's means of accepting wider responsibilities, we shall have to recognise that there are limitations to the substitution of voluntary for compulsory methods. I ask for careful thought to be given in the coming year, both to the successful carrying through of the voluntary undertakings we have given, and to the further evolution of these methods.[1]

It is not difficult to demonstrate that Sir Frederick Bain was speaking, not merely for the most authoritative trade association in Britain, but for what is perhaps the most outstanding example of an industry-wide 'peak' association in the world. Unlike most national industrial organisations, the F.B.I. claims as object and achievement

the communication and interchange of views between manufacturers and producers and the governments, govern-

[1] Sir Frederick Bain, *Presidential Address to the F.B.I. Annual General Meeting*, April 14, 1948, pp. 5–6.

ment departments, and public bodies and institutions and associations of all kinds in all parts of the world. . .[1]

With offices in eighty-five countries, the F.B.I. is represented in organisations as diverse as the British Maritime Law Association and the Royal Institute of International Affairs. F.B.I. nominees or representatives sit on thirty-four Government boards, councils and committees, and on fifty-eight committees or other bodies attached to twenty-six national and international organisations.[2]

The Federation, which employs a large and expert staff, is charged with an impressive number of functions, the scope and variety of which has tended to increase with each year. Aside from representing the F.B.I. in its relation with Government and other bodies, staff members collect, prepare, and distribute to Federation committees material on subjects as varied as international trade policy, fuel and power, patents and trade marks, smoke abatement, taxation and tariffs, to mention only a few.

Claiming to be, and widely regarded as, the ' G.H.Q. ' of British industry, the F.B.I. was regularly consulted by the Labour Government, as by its predecessors, on all matters that directly or indirectly affected the interests of industry.[3]

While the F.B.I. originated in 1917, when 124 industrial firms contributed £1,000 each to launch the organisation, its immense authority as spokesman for British industry is a product of fairly recent developments. At the beginning of the war F.B.I. membership consisted of 178 trade associations and 2,785 firms. Although this total was sufficient to give the F.B.I. status as the foremost ' peak ' trade association in Britain, it excluded a number of important industrial associations and enterprises. As has been noted, however, the vast extension of government consultation with industry during and after the war encouraged the growth of trade associations, and particularly associations that could claim to be widely representative. Moreover, at the higher levels of consultation both the Coalition and Labour Govern-

---

[1] F.B.I., *Royal Charter of Incorporation and Schedule of Bye-Laws.*

[2] These figures, and much of the following material, are based on compilations from the 30th, 31st, 32nd, 33rd, and 34th *Annual Reports* of the F.B.I., covering the years 1946–50, inclusive, particularly the 34th *Annual Report for* 1950.

[3] See Appendix II.

ments turned increasingly to the F.B.I. as representing the most influential industrial leadership and policy. As a consequence, by 1946 the F.B.I. was able to show a substantial increase in membership and as the following figures show, its post-war growth was equally impressive.

F.B.I. membership[1]

Year	Trade Associations	Firms
1946	243	4,478
		(372 new members since 1945)
1947		(678 new members 'a record for the last 25 years.')
1948	270	5,754
		(816 new members 'a new record'.)
1949	279	6,018
1950	278	6,226

In its *Annual Report* for 1948, the F.B.I. revealed that its trade association membership now included ' the representative body of the jute industry, virtually the last considerable industry hitherto unreported in the F.B.I. ', and in 1950 it was able to report membership by the National Farmers' Union. According to an F.B.I. estimate, total membership of the organisation ' represents 75 per cent of productive industry in the country '.[2]

The internal organisation of the F.B.I. reflects the dominant position within the Federation of large-scale enterprise, particularly in banking, insurance and heavy industry. Of the thirty-six persons who, in 1950, comprised the top leadership,[3] and about whom background information could be collected, nineteen, or over one-half the number, were drawn from banking, insurance, coal, and iron and steel industries. These thirty-six men held among them thirteen positions in banking, followed by insurance (9), coal (5), iron and steel (5), rubber (4), textiles (3), chemicals

[1] loc. cit.
[2] F.B.I., *The Federation of British Industries* (undated), p. 1.
Pr [3] That is, persons who were or had been by 1950 either Presidents, Vice-esidents, Deputy Presidents, or Past Presidents of the Federation.

(2), electricity (2), and other mining (1).[1] Three persons held posts in other trade associations. Firms most represented, in terms of Directorships held by F.B.I. leaders, included ; in banking, Lloyds, Midland and Barclays ; in insurance, Royal, and Phoenix ; in chemicals, Imperial Chemical Industries ; in rubber, Dunlop ; in electricity, English Electric ; in iron and steel, the Iron and Steel Federation.[2]

The governing body of the F.B.I., the Grand Council, similarly draws the bulk of its membership from the largest firms and trade associations. Reduced in size after the war,[3] the Grand Council in 1950 included one representative of each trade association member of the F.B.I., and for each two trade association representatives, one representative of the industrial and trade panels into which other F.B.I. members are grouped. By this arrangement, at any given time the Grand Council is composed of trade association representatives to the extent of two-thirds of its membership.[4]

Subsidiary to the Grand Council are the President's Advisory Committee, Finance Committee, and General Purposes Committee. The Director-General, who is directly responsible to the Council, is assisted by a Deputy Director-General and four heads of Departments, including a General Secretary, Overseas Director, Economic Director, and Technical Director. In all, the London offices of the F.B.I. are staffed by approximately sixty full-time employees, excluding clerical help, and there are, in addition, ten regional F.B.I. offices with a full-time staff of twenty-three persons.

At the same time, the Federation maintains close contact with the British Institute of Management, British Standards Institution, Chamber of Shipping, Council of Industrial Design, British Association for Commercial and Industrial Education, and the Institute of Directors. Through this system of representation and provision of services, the F.B.I. manages to co-

---

[1] The majority of F.B.I. leaders were directors in two or more of the industries listed.

[2] See Appendix II.

[3] According to the 30th *Annual Report for* 1946, the reduction was due to ' heavy growth of membership ' which would have led to a ' greatly increased Grand Council '.

[4] Based on information supplied to the writer by F.B.I. officials.

ordinate not only the interests of its members, but the interests and policies of British industry as a whole.

As has been noted, the employer counterpart of the F.B.I. is the British Employers' Confederation, the object of which is

> to safeguard the interests of all Employers within the United Kingdom of Great Britain and Ireland, by securing the fullest co-operation of their respective organisations, in dealing with all questions arising out of the relations between employers and their workpeople.[1]

Organised in 1919, the B.E.C. membership includes the employers' federations in over sixty different industries covering approximately 70 per cent of the total industrial population employed by private enterprise. It is represented on thirty-five Government Committees and bodies, and it also represents British employers before the International Labour Organisation and in the International Organisation of Employers.[2]

For many years prior to 1946, the B.E.C. and F.B.I. carried on the closest relations. The headquarters of both organisations were, and are, in the same building, and there was frequent sharing of staff and officer services.[3] Most important of all, the two organisations, while differentiated in function, had long operated a common policy on questions affecting the broad interests of industry.

Both the F.B.I. and B.E.C. maintain liaison connections with the Association of British Chambers of Commerce and the National Union of Manufacturers. The former, a federation of local Chambers of Commerce, is primarily concerned with industrial questions at local and regional levels, and the latter, whose membership consists chiefly of the smaller business concerns, exists to promote the interests of manufacturing and trading generally. Both consult regularly with the F.B.I. on matters of policy, and the F.B.I. acts as co-ordinator where, as is usual, joint or parallel action is undertaken.

Quite obviously, the considerable extension of F.B.I. authority

---

[1] B.E.C., *Constitution and Conditions of Membership* (January, 1946).
[2] B.E.C., Note on *History and Functions* (Undated pp. 1–2).
[3] For example, in 1946–47, Sir Frederick Bain, Deputy President of the F.B.I., was also Vice-President of the B.E.C.

in recent years, set against the background of the growing trade association movement, had profound implications for the Labour Government. In the first place, industry's ability ' to speak with one voice ' through ' peak ' associations considerably enhanced, as in the dispute over nationalisation of steel,[1] the effectiveness of opposition to Government policy. In the second place, as membership in associations and the influence of the F.B.I. increased, industry's demand for self-government and regulation as an alternative to Government control became more difficult to resist.

Not only was this a factor in the gradual abandonment of control in 1948–50 but it made it extremely difficult, if not impossible, for the Government to impose its own favoured form of organisation, the Development Council, on industry. The part played by the F.B.I. in co-ordinating the resistance of several industries has been attested by Harold Wilson, the Labour President of the Board of Trade :

> ' I was more than a little surprised at the sudden hostility which blew up. A hostility which in some way became infectious, covered a number of industries which had previously accepted or supported the idea and now turned against it. I do not think that this was dissociated from the special meeting called by the Federation of British Industries for the purpose of concerting the attitude of various employers' organisations to Development Councils.'[2]

Even in the clothing industry where, after a considerable struggle in the courts of law, a Council had finally been established, resistance continued. The main employers' organisation boycotted the Council and, as it was later admitted, this ' necessarily hampered the Council's work. It prevented it from ever becoming an effective central body representative of the industry as a whole '.[3] Similarly in the jewellery and silverware industry ' The Master Silversmiths Association, one of the two principal associations, has from the beginning been opposed to the Development Council '.[4]

[1] See Chapter VIII, ' The Impact of Nationalisation '.
[2] *Hansard*, December 16, 1952.
[3] Henry Strauss, Parliamentary Secretary to the Board of Trade, *Hansard*, December 16, 1952.   [4] Henry Strauss, *Hansard*, February 18, 1953.

The F.B.I. had taken its stand as early as 1947. ' The basic issue ', read the Annual Report for that year,

' is whether the Councils shall be an extension of voluntary organisations within industry or, on the other hand, an extension of the controlling and supervisory function of Government.'

Finally, as we shall now see, the growth of trade associations and the increasing concentration of industry made nonsense of Labour's attempt to carry through its anti-monopoly policy. ' Public supervision of monopolies and cartels ' was, it will be recalled, the only proposal for the private sector in the Labour Party's 1945 policy statement, *Let Us Face the Future.* It was not until 1948, however, that the Monopolies and Restrictive Practices Act received the Royal Assent, and not until 1949 that the Monopolies Commission—the investigating body set up under the Act—was appointed.

When the Labour Government fell in 1951 only two Reports, on Dental and Rainwater Goods, had been received, while four other industries were under investigation. The slow progress achieved provoked much caustic comment. ' If these six Reports,' one Labour critic complained :

' had covered industries of decent size and some importance there would perhaps have been no cause for alarm. . . But, in fact, the six cases under examination consist either of the tiniest of industries (e.g. dental goods and match making machinery) or some sub-sections of industries (e.g. cables and building castings). If future references are to consist of similar small sub-sections of industry, there will be literally hundreds of cases to be studied before any general picture can be built up ; and at the present rate of progress we should be well into the Twenty-first Century before this number of Reports can be completed.'[1]

Obviously the publication of two Reports could have little influence on the behaviour of British industry as a whole. What is surprising is that they should have had so little effect on the firms in the industries concerned. In the case of the dental

[1] C. A. R. Crosland, M.P., ' Monopoly Legislation ', *Socialist Commentary,* June, 1951.

goods industry, a Statutory Order was issued prohibiting certain restrictive practices which the Commission had condemned. This so little disturbed the Chairman of the Dental Manufacturing Company that, at the Company's following Annual General Meeting, he was able to give this assurance to shareholders :

' The position of individual manufacturers, under the Order, remains unaltered and they will be at liberty to fix and maintain their selling prices and enforce such measures as they may deem necessary to ensure that fair trading conditions are observed by their distributors. . . . Those provisions of the Dental Monopolies Order will not in any way vary or restrict your Company's trading.'[1]

In the rainwater goods industry, certain restrictive practices were condemned but no ' cease-and-desist ' order was issued. Instead the Commission recommended, and the Government accepted, that negotiations should take place between the trade associations concerned and the appropriate Government Department with a view to modifying restrictive arrangements. This method of dealing with monopoly practices set a precedent, which was to be followed in all succeeding cases by the Conservative Government. In itself it is an astonishing tribute to the influence and authority of trade associations.

The ineffectiveness of Labour's anti-monopoly policy can be traced to a number of causes. In the first place, membership of the Commission and the number of staff which it employed[2] were ludicrously small in relation to the size of the problem. In the second place the 1948 Act itself insisted that a number of separate industry studies should be completed before any general survey of restrictive practices operating throughout industry was undertaken. Not only was this procedure immensely time-consuming but it meant that prohibitory action could only be taken against practices in the industry investigated, even when it was known that the same practices were rife throughout industry. Thirdly there was no central enforcement agency and, in at least

---

[1] *Manchester Guardian*, April 3, 1951.
[2] In December, 1951, there were 10 Commissioners and a total staff of 55, *Board of Trade's Annual Report for 1951.*

one case, as subsequent Annual Reports of the Board of Trade indicated, restrictive practices continued to operate.[1]

But the real weakness of Labour's monopoly legislation stems from the fact that most monopoly practices in British industry are intimately bound up with, and in fact are enforced by, powerful trade associations. The problem of restrictive practices cannot therefore be separated from the larger problem of the control of private industrial organisations. Since trade associations played a vital part in the Labour Government's system of consultation and control it was absurd to expect that any important anti-monopoly measures could be carried through without altering the whole pattern of industry-Government relationships. Such a change, however, the Labour Government was either unwilling or unable to attempt.

But the problem of monopoly remained real and important. Although the post-war boom may well have produced some relaxation in restrictive practices, many pre-war systems of private control were known to continue, while others were merely held in abeyance.

There was evidence too that a number of cartels continued to operate, and that they were a factor in denying Britain badly needed dollar exports. Until May, 1950, for example, one of Britain's leading producers of business machines, Power-Samas, was unable to carry on business in the United States, Spain and Switzerland, through an agreement with Remington Rand.[2] On September 28, 1951, a United States Federal Court found Imperial Chemical Industries, Du Pont, and Remington Arms guilty of ' a conspiracy to divide the markets in explosives, chemicals and other products '.[3] In May, 1951, the American firm of R. Hoe and Company, manufacturers of printing presses and machinery, was indicted in New York for operating a world market-sharing agreement with two British firms.[4] In an article in December, 1949, the *Observer* reported that :

---

[1] ' It still appears that the trading policies of certain leading manufacturers (in the dental goods industry) have not to any significant extent been modified in the direction of willingness to supply new customers on trade terms, and this attitude has given rise to complaint.' *Annual Report for* 1952 : *Board of Trade.*

[2] *The Times,* May 8, 1951.

[3] *Manchester Guardian,* September 29, 1951.   [4] *Observer,* May 13, 1951.

' Officials of the State Department and E.C.A. say they have information that British firms are among those deliberately staying outside the major markets of the Western hemisphere, and so depriving Europe of desperately needed dollars and prolonging its dependence on Marshall Aid in order to honour illegal cartel agreements.[1]'

Chemical fertilisers and woodpulp were mentioned as conspicuous examples.

At the same time such evidence as is available points to growing concentration in nearly all sections of British industry. As long ago as 1935 an authoritative study[2] based on the returns of the 1935 Census of Production revealed strong monopoly trends in British industry. Measuring concentration by the percentage of all workers in an industry who were employed by the three largest firms—a form of measurement which tended to understate the degree of concentration—the following picture emerged:

CONCENTRATION OF EMPLOYMENT BY TRADE GROUPS

Trades Group	*Degree of concentration in the selected trades and subdivisons (per cent)*
Chemicals	48
Miscellaneous	47
Public utilities	44
Engineering and vehicles	43
Iron and steel	39
Food, drink and tobacco	32
Non-Ferrous metals	26
Textiles	23
Paper, printing, etc.	22
Clay and building materials	22
Leather	15
Clothing	13
Mines and quarries	10
Timber	10
Building and contracting	4
Average for all Trades	26

[1] *Observer*, December 4, 1949.
[2] H. Leak and A. Maizils, ' The Structure of British Industry ; *Journal of the Royal Statistical Society*, Vol. 108, 1945.

Since 1935 there can be no question that industrial concentration has proceeded apace. In recent years, mergers of a traditional kind have been effected in the motor-car industry, in cotton, clothing, and banking. Large multi-product concerns like Unilever, Tube Investments and Great Universal Stores have rapidly enlarged their assets, partly through natural growth but also through the acquisition of smaller firms. One important post-war monopoly trend has been the association of giant firms from what were once separate industries in the development of new industrial processes. While the joint production of nylon by Imperial Chemical Industries and Courtaulds, the rayon manufacturers, and the foundation of the new petro-chemical industry through the association of the principal oil and chemical companies, are the most conspicuous examples, many other illustrations of what one P.E.P. study[1] calls ' joint enterprise ' can be found.

These developments have, of course, great significance. Apart from enhancing the capacity of industry to operate, should the economic climate change, the kind of restrictionist policies that had characterised the 1930s it is fair to say that the growth of industrial concentration and of trade associations sensibly alters the balance of power between Government and industry and must greatly circumscribe the effective authority of the State. Now that the apparatus of war-time controls has been largely dismantled, Labour's need for a new industrial policy which will permit a measure of positive regulation of the private sector has become urgent.

But as far as can be seen, Labour in opposition is as far from finding such a policy as it was in office.

[1] *P.E.P. Broadsheet,* ' The Structure of Industry ', Vol. XIX, No. 350, January, 1953.

CHAPTER V

INDUSTRY AND LABOUR

' A great society is one in which businessmen think
greatly of their functions.'

Whitehead.

It is undoubtedly no coincidence that what sociologists and
psychologists call ' the human factor ' in industry began to be
noted, in Britain, at about the same time as trade unions and the
Labour Party became an important element in politics. Until
the First World War, at any rate, the worker was regarded less
as a human than a commodity factor, as subject to the laws of
demand and supply as cotton cloth or wheat. The aged, the
infirm, and the unemployed among the working class could be
aided, in piecemeal fashion, by the State, and trade unions could
attempt to represent the interests of the rest, but the results,
whether wage increases or welfare legislation, were more a
product of economic coercion than of social enlightenment. And
where enlightenment was given conscious articulation in politics,
by a Gladstone or a Disraeli, a Joseph Chamberlain or a Lloyd
George, the accent was typically British. Liberalism and Tory
democracy, not Marxism, were the authentic voices of reform and
progress.

In the main, extreme assumptions about class struggle and
warfare could be and were regarded as questionable foreign
importations, even by the working class. In Britain at the end
of the nineteenth century, there were only 1,250,000 trade unionists affiliated to the Trades Union Congress, and the membership
of the Fabian Society, Social Democratic Federation, and the
other socialist organisations combined totalled not more than a
few thousand. Working-class consciousness was about to take a
political direction as 1900 approached, but it did not yet threaten
the interests of property.

By the end of the First World War, however, the climate had radically changed. From two members in 1900 the Parliamentary Labour Party had risen to 63 in 1918, and it was to reach 138 four years later.[1] T.U.C. ranks, meanwhile, had swelled to 4,532,000. Membership in the Labour Party increased from 376,000 in 1900 to more than 3 million in 1918, and that same year it issued a sweeping manifesto, largely drafted by Sidney Webb, proposing the nationalisation of the land, railways, mines and electric power.[2] Unrest and dissatisfaction were widespread in industrial areas; indeed, in the six years after the war the number of man days lost through strikes and lock-outs reached the staggering total of 187,580,000.[3] Clearly, as the Whitley Commission noted, ' a permanent improvement in relations must be founded upon something other than a cash basis.'

In the two decades after the war numerous attempts were made to achieve such an improvement. The sociology of the factory was closely studied in an effort to isolate the ingredients of a harmonious work environment. Schemes for the perfection of conciliation and arbitration machinery were developed and applied. Profit-sharing and co-partnership made their appearance in an attempt to give the workers a share of the status and security of property ownership. Joint consultation was extended throughout industry. Although such devices fell off markedly during the depression years they reappeared with new vigour in the years after the Second World War. Indeed the Welfare State itself is to a large extent an attempt to establish an industrial society ' upon something other than a cash basis '.

The war years, involving a labour shortage and the allocation of manpower and resources, had witnessed a notable expansion of tripartite consultation among industry, labour and Government. The Labour Government was to make refinements and improvements but not to alter the basic structure of labour-management relations. Existing machinery of collective bargaining, joint consultation, arbitration and conciliation were to be extended and

[1] The Times, House of Commons 1951 (London, 1951), p. 24.
[2] Labour and the New Social Order (London, 1918), pp. 13–15.
[3] Alfred Robens, Minister of Labour, quoted in the Financial Times, September 17, 1951. By contrast, the total number of man days lost through strikes and lock-outs in the same period after World War Two was 12,740,000.

perfected. Specifically, the Government was to reject a wage policy for the whole of industry, and workers' control for the nationalised sector. In other words, the Labour Government was to continue a pattern of development that had begun a very long time before. Full employment itself, however, brought important changes in industrial relationships. Historically, a reserve of unemployment had enabled management to establish the terms and conditions of work, although these rights had been somewhat limited by trade unionism.

Full employment, of course, involves a shift of power in the direction of the workers; or, to put it another way, under full employment the 'fear of the sack' can no longer be the chief means of keeping industrial discipline. As regards labour, new incentives must be found to achieve stability and efficiency. The employer, at the same time, must radically alter his psychology. In a period of job plenty success belongs, *a priori*, to the employer who can keep his work force, not to the one who can dismiss it.

It is not surprising therefore that the post-war period was marked by a growing interest in management techniques. In 1947 the British Institute of Management was formed to promote management studies and to represent the interests of professional management. The Labour Government's view of the role of management and the importance of a new approach may be judged by the fact that the B.I.M. was partly supported by Government funds,[1] and in fact developed from the recommendations of the Committee of Enquiry appointed by Sir Stafford Cripps, to advise on ' the steps which should be taken to form a central institution for all questions of management. . . .' While the confident assertion that industry had ' moved away from the authoritarian conception of the " Managerial Revolution " which was popular a few years ago ',[2] may be doubted, it was largely agreed that the effects of full employment were to greatly relax traditional work discipline and to introduce a new atmosphere into industry.

This new relationship was not, however, accompanied by

[1] £150,000 over a 5-year period.
[2] Sir Stafford Cripps, in his speech at the Inaugural Meeting of the British Institute of Management, April 21, 1948.

radical instutional changes towards democracy in industry. The idea of workers' control, meaning the election or appointment of workers' *representatives* to Boards of Directors, had been rejected by pre-war Labour Party conferences and found no expression in the organisation of the new nationalised industries. Moreover neither the Labour Government, industry nor organised labour, with some exceptions, actively encouraged workers' participation in management. On behalf of the Government Sir Stafford Cripps declared, in 1946, that

> ' there is not yet a very large number of workers in Britain capable of taking over large enterprises. I have on many occasions tried to get representatives of the workers on all sorts of bodies and working parties. It has always been extremely difficult to get enough people who are qualified to do that sort of job, and, until there has been more experience by the workers of the managerial side of industry, I think it would be almost impossible to have worker-controlled industry in Britain, even if it were on the whole desirable.'[1]

A somewhat similar position was taken by Sir Robert Sinclair, President of the F.B.I., in an address to the British Institute of Management in 1950.

> ' There is no room in the chain of authority for someone who is representative of a group. . . . I know there is a desire for special training of T.U. members. If that means representation of T.U. members on management, then I do not agree with it. If it means that, as individuals, they are trained to fit themselves individually to take more responsibility in the conduct of business or to understand its problems, that is fine.'[2]

The industry view was well summarised by the Chairman of the Dunlop Rubber Company in 1947. 'A share in management,' he stated, ' is not a right to be demanded, but a distinction to be earned and a responsibility to be borne.'[3]

[1] Quoted in *The Times*, October 28, 1946.
[2] Sir Robert Sinclair, Summary of Address to the Harrogate Conference of the B.I.M., *The Manager*, Vol. 18, No. 12 (December, 1950), pp. 592–595.
[3] Quoted in *The Times*, May 6, 1947.

As early as 1944, the T.U.C., in its Interim Report on Post-war Reconstruction,[1] had maintained that the trade unions should keep independent of executive authority. At the Labour Party Conference in 1948, during a heated discussion of a resolution calling for ' workers' participation through their Trade Unions in the direction and management of nationalised industry at all levels,' Will Lawther, President of the National Union of Mineworkers, declared that

> ' We as a miners' organisation do not want to have people in the ridiculous position that we see on the Continent where the president or secretary of a miners' organisation is also on the Coal Board running the industry, so that he has on occasion to pass a resolution to ask himself to give himself something. . . . The position of the Trade Union is to remain independent of the Coal Board and independent of whatever Boards of Executives may be set up .'[2]

The resolution, although supported by the Amalgamated Engineering Union, the Association of Engineering and Shipbuilding Draughtsmen, the Union of Post Office Workers and the National Union of Railwaymen, was finally withdrawn, and there was no subsequent revision by the T.U.C. of its 1944 position.

Trade union leaders who were appointed to the Boards of nationalised industries served, it should be noted, not in a representative but in an individual capacity, as persons who were ' experienced in the organisation of workers '—one of the statutory qualifications for membership. In 1951, only 9 of the 47 full-time members, and 7 of 48 part-time members of the Boards of the nationalised industries were trade unionists, and five of the Boards—British Overseas Airways, British European Airways, Hotels Executive, Road Passenger Executive, and the Gas Board —had no trade unionist among their full-time members.[3] ' There is thus,' said one impartial report on the nationalised industries, ' a considerable measure of factual basis for the employees' complaint that " the old gang " is still in power.'[4]

[1] Reprinted as Appendix D, *76th Annual Report of the T.U.C.*, pp. 393–442.
[2] *Report of the 47th Annual Conference of the Labour Party*, (Scarborough, 1948), p. 170.
[3] Acton Society Trust, *The Men on the Boards : A Study of the Composition of the Boards of Nationalised Industry*. No. 4 (1951), pp. 6–9.   [4] ibid., p. 12.

Yet such rank-and-file criticism of the management personnel in nationalised industries did not lead to much action to prepare union members for managerial roles. The argument, advanced by Cripps and others, that workers were not capable of taking over large enterprises may be granted. But it does not explain why, apart from the limited training and promotion schemes operated by the nationalised industries, so little was done to provide workers with training and experience for future participation in management. Although it was frequently suggested that the trade unions join together to establish university chairs in ' production engineering and management ', and supply scholarships to members to attend courses,[1] few such steps were taken. At the end of 1951, not one trade union representative had attended any of the sessions of the Administrative Staff College, established in 1946 ' for young executives in private enterprise and officials in the public services and trade unions,'[2] and providing ' a course of studies which investigates the principles and techniques of organisation and administration in civil life '.[3] While the T.U.C. gave support to three trade union-related educational organisations, the Workers' Educational Association, the National Council of Labour Colleges, and Ruskin College, none of these were primarily management training institutions.[4]

The Clapham educational centre, organised by the T.U.C. in 1951, ' to give a good grounding in the principles of factory organisation and work study, costing and wage systems ',[5] was designed to help trade union officials to carry out their duties— as union officials—more effectively. As *The Times Review of Industry* was later to assure its readers.

' it is important to recognise that trade union technical training schemes and programmes are not designed with the ulterior motive of enabling trade unions to take over management functions and responsibilities. They do not,

---

[1] *Hansard*, Vol. 467, Col. 935, July 15, 1951.
[2] *Economist*, November 10, 1945.
[3] Administrative Staff College *Handbook* (1951), p. 7.
[4] Allan Flanders, *British Trade Unionism* (Bureau of Current Affairs, London, 1948), p. 53.
[5] T.U.C. *What the T.U.C. Is Doing* (Spring, 1951), p. 30.

indeed, indicate any departure from the traditional union role of safeguarding and advancing the interests of members.'[1]

Although management training was largely neglected, considerable attention was paid to extending the scope and functions of joint consultation. Joint consultation, which may be simply defined as regular and systematic discussion by employers and employees of matters of common interest,[2] can be an important device for the creation and maintenance of harmonious industrial relations. It provides, in the first place, a means for the discussion of problems that arise from the actual work environment, and for the exchange of information and points of view. Minor grievances on either side that, potentially, could be causes of breakdown may be thoroughly explored with a view toward an orderly settlement. Finally, joint consultation, by regularly bringing together the two sides of industry, promotes mutual understanding and respect. In other words, it is concerned not only with the settlement of disputes before they become crucial, but with the attitudes that underlie and frequently give rise to, disputes.

As was the case with other types of industrial relations machinery,

' The last war gave an added impetus to the establishment of joint consultation by way of Joint Production Committees, or their equivalent, particularly in the engineering, shipbuilding, coalmining and building and civil engineering industries, where a large number of committees were set up for the specific purpose of aiding production.'[3]

On the value of joint consultation in the post-war period

[1] *The Times Review of Industry*, ' Trade Union Specialists in Management Techniques ', November, 1954.

[2] The term ' joint consultation ' covers a wide variety of consultative machinery including works councils, joint consultation councils, works consultative committees, works committees, policy committees, or joint production committees. On joint consultation in general see *The Times Review of Industry*, ' Joint Consultation ', May, 1950, and Ministry of Labour and National Service, *Industrial Relations Handbook* : *Supplement No. 3*.

[3] Ministry of Labour and National Service, ' Joint Consultation in Industry ' *Industrial Relations Handbook* : *Supplement No. 3*, December, 1949, p. 4.

business opinion was divided. There were employers who, as *The Times* noted, in January 1947

> ' Regard joint consultation as an infringement of their prerogative of management, as the cause of discontent among their foremen, as an opportunity for trouble-makers, or simply as a waste of time ; they are disinclined to take suggestions from their workers seriously and reluctant to take them into their confidence.'[1]

A better way of teaching workers a sense of common purpose was, in the view of some business men

> ' to begin at the beginning—with the young people—all of them, not merely the outstanding five or ten per cent—as they come into industry for the first time. . . . by arranging for them such a systematic, regular and progressive education and training as will enable them to grow up not merely understanding but proud of their work, of industry, and of the social purpose both serve.'[2]

Much thought was given to the position of junior managers, foremen and supervisors, whose authority was seen to be undermined indirectly by full employment and, more directly, by joint consultation. At the end of the period the Anglo-American Productivity Team Report on the Training of Supervisors was to recommend as a matter of urgency, the raising of the status and rewards of junior management.[3]

There were others, however, who saw that through joint consultation the antagonisms and hostilities of an industrial order could be replaced by mutual co-operation, stopping short at the level of direction and decision-making. As put by one industrialist, the function of joint consultation is

> ' ultimately to get rid of the division of factories into " bosses and the rest " which still colours the background thinking of most people.'[4]

[1] *The Times*, January 8, 1947.
[2] Letter to *The Times*, H. E. G. West, Chairman and Managing Director of Newton, Chambers and Co., Ltd.
[3] *Anglo-American Productivity Team Report*, November 1951.
[4] Quoted in *The Times*, May 20, 1947.

On one thing, however, business opinion was united. Whether industry is publicly or privately owned

' its directors must be appointed by and answerable to the owners not to the workers. The owners or their representatives must have the last word on policy ; they must appoint managers, who must enjoy authority to give binding orders.'[1]

On the side of the workers there were also diverse views. There were those who regard joint consultation

' as a trap ; there are shop stewards who dislike the restriction of responsibility or decline in popularity which such a committee sometimes involves for them ; there are union branch officials who fear encroachment upon their negotiating rights.'[2]

For others joint consultation involved the rather modest ambition of having a closer look at the company's accounts. In yet another view, joint consultation means ' some measure of self-government in industry ' ;[3] while according to another, and more authoritative opinion, joint consultation

' means the participation of all in the running of the industry in which they are employed. It means the abandonment, as we move forward into our new, socialist, society of the outmoded and frustrating two-sidedness of industry ; for industry is a group activity and co-operation is its lifeblood. If industry is anaemic, socialism cannot be a success. It is thus vital for the manager and essential for the socialist to develop consultation to the full without delay.'[4]

In practice, of course, most joint consultation schemes in British industry, involved little participation by workers in policy-making, and the majority of schemes restricted participation to relatively minor matters for decision. Joint consultative

---

[1] *The Times,* May 20, 1947.
[2] *The Times,* January 8, 1947.
[3] Bernard Sullivan, union representative, commenting on joint consultation at Rego Clothiers, Ltd., *Tottenham and Edmonton Herald,* June 10, 1949.
[4] *Management by Consent,* Report of a Committee appointed jointly by the Association of Supervisory Staffs, Executives and Technicians and the Fabian Society (Fabian Research Studies, No. 125, May, 1948).

committees usually consisted of an equal number of employees' representatives and nominees of the firm, with a senior official of the firm as chairman and joint secretaries. Topics most often discussed were the health, safety and welfare of employees, grievances, interpretation of rules and regulations, discipline with special reference to absenteeism, maximum utilisation of plant, economy in the use of raw materials, the elimination of defective work, and improvement in methods of production. Frequently additional subjects for discussion were referred to joint consultative committees by management. Thus the *Works Handbook* at Samual Fox and Co., Ltd., states that

> ' Formal meetings shall take place between representatives of the management and of the workmen for the purpose of discussing matters of production and welfare together with certain aspects of Company policy which in the opinion of management can be usefully discussed.'

In other cases, the functions of consultative committees are listed in detail. At the Southern United Telephone Cables, Ltd., the duties of the Joint Works Committee are set forth as

(*a*) General Welfare and comfort of employees ;
(*b*) Accident Prevention and first-aid facilities ;
(*c*) Interpretation of works rules and regulations ;
(*d*) Time-keeping ;
(*e*) Operation of wage rates excluding the fixing of general rates dealt with on a National or District basis ;
(*f*) Canteen arrangements ;
(*g*) Benevolent fund ;
(*h*) Other Charity Collections ;
(*i*) Election of sub-committees.

The *Handbook* further states that the Committee Chairman ' shall be a member of management ', and that the Company's Personnel Officer shall act as Secretary.[1]

Attempts to extend the scope of these and other joint consultative agreements were only partly successful. Following the almost national discussion of the functions of joint consultation

[1] Southern United Telephone Cables, Ltd. *Works Handbook*, 1950, pp. 10–11.

in the press and elsewhere during 1947–48, the Labour Government, trade unions and industry made an effort to promote consultative arrangements in industries which had formerly lacked such machinery. By August, 1948, a census taken by the Ministry of Labour and National Service showed that of 54 industries, 38 were operating some type of formal joint consultation, including the nationalised industries which were required by law to provide the necessary machinery. In November, 1949, the Ministry of Labour and National Service submitted to employers' and workers' organisations a proposal that the Ministry should take up the question of joint consultation directly with firms. The proposal was attacked, particularly by the British Employers' Confederation, on the grounds that it introduced a measure of coercion into a hitherto voluntary relationship, and it was eventually withdrawn. In its place, the B.E.C. asked its employer federation members to ' review the position '.[1]

In the period 1945–51 somewhat more success was achieved in another, related, area of employer-worker relations ; one which, in the long run, can be more significant for industrial harmony than joint consultation. Unlike joint consultation, which ultimately threatens the position of the managers, profit-sharing and co-partnership, by which the workers become dividend recipients and part owners of industry,[2] represent concessions on the part of the shareholders. Such concessions, of course, can easily be made by managers who, in this respect, have quite a different point of view to the owners. Profit-sharing, in the first place, depends on a reasonably stable level of profits over a long-term period, and is therefore most successfully practised by firms who enjoy a monopoly or quasi-monopoly position.[3] In these

[1] British Employers' Confederation, 30*th Annual Report*, 1949–50, p. 10.

[2] According to the Ministry of Labour and National Service, ' The term " profit sharing " applies to those cases in which an employer agrees with his employees that they shall receive, in partial remuneration of their labour, and in addition to their wages, a share, fixed beforehand, in the profits realised by the undertakings to which the Profit-Sharing Scheme relates '. Co-partnership has been defined, by the Industrial Co-partnership Association, as ' an extension of profit-sharing whereby the worker accumulates his share of the profits in the capital of the business and thus becomes a shareholder '.

[3] The *Financial Times* noted in one of a series of articles on profit-sharing, November 6, 1946, that ' Industries which are stable and possibly sheltered from outside competition ' are those in which profit-sharing is most likely to succeed.

cases profit-sharing is an effective device for attracting and keeping a labour force,[1] and it tends to give the industrial giants a substantial advantage in the competition for workers which is one characteristic of full employment. Finally, profit-sharing appeals to managers as a means of capturing the loyalty of the workers not only in one plant or industry but in society as a whole. ' I look on profit-sharing ', declared the Chairman of the woollen cloth manufacturing firm of J. T. and J. Taylor, ' as the abolition of war between the classes.'[2]   According to another industry spokesman, ' England must move in this direction or be swallowed up by nationalisation or Communism '.[3]   To the Chairman and Managing Director of the Rugby Portland Cement Company, the merit of profit-sharing is that it ' closely identifies the interests of the employees with those of the shareholders '.   There can be no profit-sharing or dividends unless, of course, there are profits.[4]

The possible political effects of such identity of interests did not go unnoticed by the major political parties.   Ernest Marples, Conservative M.P., argued in 1947 that co-partnership presented the only real alternative to Labour Socialism,[5] and Conservative opinion identified with R. A. Butler, David Eccles, and Lord Hailsham (Quintin Hogg) has long accepted the principle of profit-sharing and co-partnership in industry.   Indeed, Winston Churchill himself, at the Conservative Party Conference in October, 1946, declared on the Party's behalf that

> ' Our Conservative aim is to build a property-owning demo-
> cracy, both independent and inter-dependent.   In this I
> include profit-sharing in suitable industries and intimate
> consultation between employers and wage-earners.   In fact,
> we seek so far as possible to make the status of the wage-

---

[1] It was precisely for this reason that, in 1951, the Federation of Master Cotton Spinners' Associations, whose membership largely reflects small-scale enterprise, rejected profit-sharing, and, again, it was largely for this reason that a number of its members chose to resign from the Federation rather than give up the practice.

[2] *Yorkshire Observer*, September 29, 1950.

[3] Managing Director of British Waste, Ltd., quoted in *British Rayon and Silk Journal*, January, 1951, p. 51.

[4] Quoted in the *Financial Times*, June 13, 1950.

[5] *The Road to Prosperity* (London, 1947), pp. 13–19.

earner that of a partner rather than that of an irresponsible employee.'[1]

While the Liberal Party has always been closely identified with the profit-sharing movement, it became committed to compulsory profit-sharing only in 1949. Whether because co-partnership ' put out the right way, could win back the working man's vote ',[2] or because the alternative ' is between Partnership and Socialism. There is no other choice ',[3] the Liberal Party proposals were a good deal more extreme than those advanced by the other parties. In 1949 the Party declared that if elected to form a government, it would introduce legislation requiring every industrial concern with over 50 workers and/or £50,000 of capital to introduce a scheme that would provide, among other things, for the sharing of surplus earnings between workers and shareholders after dividends and reserves had been provided for, and for the encouragement of employee shareholding and representation on Boards of Directors.[4]

Trade union and Labour Party circles, traditionally hostile to profit-sharing, showed increasing interest in such schemes on the theory that profit-sharing and co-partnership would further democratise industry. Among leading trade unionists, Lincoln Evans, General Secretary of the Iron and Steel Trades Confederation and member of the T.U.C. General Council, Captain Mark Hewitson, M.P. and a leading official of the General & Municipal Workers' Union,[5] and A. C. C. Robertson, President of the United Textile Factory Workers' Association,[6] were advocates of profit-sharing. It was especially significant that at

---

[1] Quoted in *Financial Times*, November 11, 1946. Two days after Churchill spoke the *Manchester Guardian* editorially commented : ' It is difficult to believe that the motives behind the Conservative Party's sudden interest in profit-sharing are entirely altruistic. To begin thinking of it not in the heyday of power and opportunity but only when the party is in obvious need of what is called " a constructive alternative to Socialism " suggested that Sir David Maxwell Fyfe's " empirical approach " is working overtime.' October 7, 1946.

[2] Walter James, " Co-partnership in Industry ', *Fortnightly*, April, 1948.

[3] Elliot Dodds, quoted in *Daily Mail*, March 16, 1949.

[4] Liberal Party, *People in Industry : A Report on the Liberal Co-ownership Proposals* (London, 1949).

[5] In September, 1950, Hewitson representing the employees negotiated a profit-sharing agreement with Tate and Lyle, Ltd.

[6] Robertson called for profit-sharing in the textile industry in a speech reported in the *Manchester Evening Chronicle*, April 27, 1950.

I

the Trades Union Congress in September, 1951, Hugh Gaitskell could suggest, with reference to the unequal distribution of wealth, that

> ' We should not exclude altogether from our considerations as one possible contribution to its solution some form of partnership by the workers in individual firms or industries, through, for example, the distribution of bonus shares reflecting the rise in undistributed profits. I throw it out as an idea which you can chew over.'[1]

As the *Economist* noted, the proposal was

> ' Greeted without enthusiasm, but with some flicker of interest. That is significant enough. A few years ago it would have certainly have been howled down. . . . It is perhaps a measure of mental bankruptcy rather than flexibility that the search should have led, however tentatively, to the familiar and essentially capitalist notion of profit-sharing .'[2]

The generally favourable opinion of profit-sharing was reflected in the increase in the number of operating schemes in industry. While before the war profit-sharing was relatively negligible, involving only about 2 per cent of all workers, unofficial estimates in 1950 placed the total involvement at between 10 and 15 per cent of the total work force. Firms practising profit-sharing and/or co-partnership included many of Britain's most important and leading industrial establishments : Associated Portland Cement, the Nuffield Organisation, Thomas Hedley, Lever Brothers, Spillers, Tate and Lyle, Montague Burton, Reckitt and Colman, Clarke Nicholls and Coombe, Joseph Lucas, Triplex and Kodak.[3]

The popularity of profit-sharing and co-partnership, however, is not necessarily evidence of increasing democratisation in British industry. While such schemes create an appearance of workers' participation in the ownership and profits of industry, it is, in most cases, without substance. In the first place, profits

[1] *T.U.C. Report of the* 83*rd Annual Congress*, Blackpool, September, 1951, p. 368.
[2] September 15, 1951.
[3] Since the fall of the Labour Government in October 1951, there has been no abatement of profit-sharing in industry. In 1954, I.C.I. and Courtaulds started up profit-sharing schemes.

are usually shared only after the real profits have already been reduced by provisions for the preference shares, a basic dividend on the ordinary shares, and reserves. The surplus then remaining is somewhat unequally divided between shareholders and employees.

As far as control is concerned, in only a fraction of cases can the workers acquire enough shares to give them even an important minority interest, and in most cases employee-owned shares do not carry voting rights.

The significance of profit-sharing and co-partnership is not to be found in the additional income such schemes provide, or in the measure of workers' control which such schemes make possible. The principal impact of partnership proposals is at the psychological level where the aim, from the standpoint of industry, is no less than the creation of a new industrial psychology. Objectively, it can be argued that the workers' share of profits and control in industry is more illusion than reality, but if workers embrace the illusion it can have profound political and social effects. It is almost axiomatic that any identification of interests between the workers and private enterprise operates against an identification of interests between the workers and socialism, and ultimately, between the workers and the State. In Labour circles, the rationalisation of profit-sharing and co-partnership is often in terms of the effects on productivity and the addition to wages. But, as the *Financial Times* pointed out in 1946 :

> ' It is doubtful whether profit-sharing and co-partnership can be considered as a great incentive towards increased output or the reduction of waste and spoilt work. The addition of 6 per cent to earnings—the average for all schemes in 1937, although some individual schemes paid substantially more—is not by itself much of a stimulus, especially when it is subject to income tax.'

The real importance of such schemes, it went on to say, lay in the ' increased loyalty and contentment ' of the labour force employed.[1]

Similarly with joint consultation. The achievement of ex-

[1] *Financial Times*, November 6, 1946.

tended joint consultation is not so much that the workers become active participants in management with a decisive influence on the policies of the firm, but that the workers, by being consulted, by being given information of a confidential character, by coming to know on a personal basis the senior personnel of industry,[1] begin to share the psychology, values, and outlook of the property-owning and controlling class. Perhaps the majority of British workers, as has been suggested, do not, in fact, believe in workers' control of industry.[2] But a share of the status and dignity that comes with a relationship to ownership and control is an objective that the working class, understandably, is unwilling to reject. Principally for this reason, profit-sharing, co-partnership and joint consultation can be expected to be increasingly popular and more widely practised in Britain.

At the same time, the opportunity presented to British industry is clear and attractive. There is, without doubt, considerable insight in the numerous observations that profit-sharing and co-partnership are alternatives to socialism and nationalisation, to class war and Communism. As the *Financial Times* put it :

> ' by demonstrating the common interest which both workers and management have in the efficient running of industry, it should help to bring to an end the sterile debate over nationalisation which bedevils politics today.'[3]

It is directly relevant to the point that firms in industries[4] marked

---

[1] Thus an account of a ' successful ' joint consultation scheme in the chemical industry by a union representative states : ' We have held monthly meetings to consider all questions to do with production . . . and even profits to see how much of each pound goes into the carve-up. These representatives have to give an understanding not to disclose any financial data in a particular case. These firms, after objecting to it—I had to take one or two people out to get them gay and goofy— were prepared to agree to a constitution which is being applied on a wider and wider scale in the chemistry industry.' Representatives of the Chemical Workers' Union at the 1946 T.U.C. Congress, quoted in M. P. Fogarty, ' Conclusion ', *Joint Consultation*: *A Symposium*. Industrial Welfare Society, July, 1948, p. 71.

[2] A survey taken by Social Surveys, Ltd., in 1950, of workers' opinion in industry showed that only 48 per cent of respondents thought that they and their ' mates ought to share in the management ' of the firm. Thirty per cent thought that they should not share in management, and 22 per cent were undecided. ' What Do Workers Think ? ' *Future*, Vol. 5, No. 3 (June–July, 1950).

[3] *Financial Times*, May 21, 1945.

[4] E.g. Tate and Lyle in 1950, after *Labour Believes in Britain* had proposed nationalisation of the sugar refining industry ; I.C.I. in 1954 after *Challenge to Britain* had proposed nationalisation of sections of the chemical industry.

down for public ownership in recent Labour Party policy statements have responded with the introduction of profit-sharing schemes. The impact of these moves, on public opinion in general and on the trade unions directly concerned in particular, should not be underrated.

Meanwhile, a poll of workers' opinion in 1950, reported by *Future Magazine*, showed

> ' that there is a very high degree of contentment and confidence in management on the part of the work people, but it also shows that there is still much educative work to be done, and that notions about workers sharing management are making headway. . . . It would seem that management has to tackle the *total* environment if the worker is to be kept contented and loyal.'[1]

The opportunity, as well as the perils of the missed chance, were perhaps summed up as well as they could be in a symposium on joint consultation conducted by the Industrial Welfare Society in July, 1948. 'The importance of this subject ', a participant wrote, ' is self-evident ', for as G. M. Trevelyan wrote in *English Social History*—' If the French Noblesse had been capable of playing cricket with their peasants, their chateaux would never have been burnt '.[2]

[1] *Future Magazine*, June–July, 1950, ' What Do Workers Think ? ' p. 19.
[2] Richard Davies, in *Joint Consultation : A Symposium*, p. 6.

CHAPTER VI

INDUSTRY AND TAXATION

When the Labour Government came to power in 1945 it was confronted by a dilemma as old as democracy, a dilemma, moreover, particularly crucial in the Welfare State. For the ancient problem of whether freedom and equality are compatible values in society is given a special urgency by the success of a political movement whose attachment to freedom is no less enduring than its devotion to ' fair shares '. Freedom has traditionally meant, besides political freedom, freedom to make the best of one's opportunities, freedom to rise in the social and economic order, freedom to acquire wealth and pass on that wealth to one's children. Equality under democratic socialism, on the other hand, has always been defined as a rejection of ' the claims of the few to live on the labour of the many ', a demand that ' fair shares should be the national rule '.[1] As was noted in *Labour and the New Social Order* (1918)

> ' The first principle of the Labour Party—in significant contrast with those of the Capitalist System, whether expressed by the Liberal or by the Conservative Party—is the securing to every member of the community, in good times and bad alike (and not only to the strong and able, the well-born and the fortunate), of all the requisites of healthy life and worthy citizenship.'

Conservatives, of course, have long argued the incompatibility of freedom and equality, and in Britain since 1945 have stressed that the dilemma could be, and was, resolved only at the expense of freedom.

To the Labour Government, however, the conflict between ' fair shares ' and certain freedoms associated with *laisser-faire* was less important than problems arising from the pursuit of a ' fair shares ' policy in a mixed economy. It is a truism that incentives in a mixed economy are not fundamentally different from those

[1] *Labour and the New Society* (1950), p. 4.

that operate in a capitalist system.[1] This is not to suggest that Government exhortation and appeal, the loyalty of trade unionists to political leaders, and industrial policy that takes its lead from the Government are not without effect ; but the principal and most powerful incentive remains the wage-and-profit motive. Inevitably, therefore, a policy of income redistribution in a predominantly capitalist economy is bound to meet with various forms of opposition from affected interests ; and the extent of the opposition is closely related to the severity of the taxes imposed.

There can be no doubt that the Labour Government carried redistributive taxation and fair shares considerably further than was thought either possible or desirable by most financial authorities. Between 1945 and 1951 the higher incomes were taxed much more heavily than they had been during the war.[2] Combined rates of surtax and income tax reached 19s. 6d. in the pound on incomes of £20,000 a year and more, and in effect imposed a ceiling on post-tax incomes of a little more than £6,000. In addition, taxes on inheritance and purchase tax—which fell most heavily on luxury and semi-luxury goods—were greatly increased. The largest tax increases, however, fell on business profits. By 1951

---

[1] Thus, for example, when Labour Ministers decided the level of directors' salaries in the new nationalised industries regard had to be paid to current payments in private industry, for fear that the most qualified persons might not be forthcoming.

[2] As the following figures show, the Labour Government made a slight reduction from the war-time level of the standard rate of income taxation on incomes below £2,000 per annum ; in addition, exemptions and allowances were increased. Surtax rates, however, were increased.

Year	Income Tax Standard Rate (shillings and pence in the pound)	Range of Income (£'s)	Surtax Rates of Tax 1939–46	1946–49
1940–41	8–6	2,000– 2,500	2–0	2–0
1941–42	10–0	2,500– 3,000	2–3	2–6
1942–43	10–0	3,000– 4,000	3–3	3–6
1943–44	10–0	4,000– 5,000	4–3	4–6
1944–45	10–0	5,000– 6,000	5–0	5–6
1945–46	10–0	6,000– 8,000	5–9	6–6
1946–47	9–0	8,000–10,000	7–0	7–6
1947–48	9–0	10,000–12,000	8–3	8–6
1948–49	9–0	12,000–15,000	8–3	9–6
1949–50	9–0	15,000–20,000	9–0	10–0
1950–51	9–0	Over 20,000	9–6	10–0
1951–52	9–6			

Source : *Reports of the Commissioners of H.M. Inland Revenue,* 1945 to 1951. (H.M.S.O.).

profits tax[1] had been raised to 10% on undistributed profits and to as much as 50% on dividends, the remaining net profit being further taxed at the standard rate of income tax, i.e., at 9s. 6d. in the pound. The restriction of distributed profits by discriminatory taxation was further reinforced after 1948 by annual appeals to the Federation of British Industries and boards of directors for ' dividend restraint '. In 1951, when voluntary restraint was abandoned, the Labour Government prepared legislation which would have imposed a statutory limitation on dividends.[2]

In the event it is scarcely surprising that the export of capital and tax avoidance became increasingly serious problems ; indeed, in 1949 it was suggested, with reference to the balance of payments, that ' the first item which is likely to suggest itself as a factor aggravating our difficulties, is the export of capital '.[3] The whole question of capital export was, of course, bound up with the genuine and partly encouraged investment in Commonwealth and colonial development, and cannot be entirely separated from it. It was difficult to know, for example, whether in a particular case large-scale expansion of a business subsidiary abroad had as its ulterior purpose the avoidance of Exchequer control, or whether it was primarily intended to raise living standards in a backward area, or earn more dollars for the United Kingdom. Similarly the migration of a particular enterprise abroad, to the extent that it shifted the locus of taxation and was followed by the actual plant and machinery, was welcomed by native authorities, although such a move might have been principally designed to escape British taxation.

Estimates of the totals of private capital export 1945–51 must, of necessity, be imprecise since the official figures do not distinguish between public and private capital export. The volume

[1] In 1947 the Labour Government substituted for the war-time Excess Profits Tax a Profits Tax which was charged at two rates : 10 per cent on undistributed profits and 25 per cent on distributed profits. In 1949 the tax on distributed profits was raised to 30 per cent and in 1951 it was further raised to 50 per cent. See *Reports of the Commissioners of H.M. Inland Revenue*, 1945 to 1951. H.M.S.O.

[2] *Control of Dividends*, Cmd. 8318, July 1951. The Labour Government was defeated at the October 1951 General Election before a Bill based on the White Paper could be introduced.

[3] Lionel Robbins, ' The Sterling Problem ', *Lloyds Bank Review*, October, 1949, pp. 5–7.

of investment by private companies in subsidiaries abroad is therefore unknown although available information suggests that such investment was, in fact, sizeable. For example, in 1947–48 United Kingdom private investment in Australia totalled £24,400,000.[1] In 1949, 107 subsidiary or associate chemical companies were operating abroad, and the formation of 47 more was ' at present under contemplation '.[2] From 1946 to 1950 a total of 34 United Kingdom firms began operations in Canada ;[3] and throughout the period there was a considerable investment in subsidiaries in South Africa, Australia, Egypt, Malta and elsewhere by British cement and textile firms,[4] particularly.

Illegal export of capital, mainly by under-valuing exports and overpayment for imports, was estimated by one observer at hardly less than £200 million in 1946–49.[5] Attempts to avoid exchange control assumed at times, dangerous proportions. Before the devaluation of the £ in 1949, rumours of which had been pending for some time, there had been a determined and generally successful attempt by market operators to 'get into' gold and dollars either in their liquid forms or in the shape of securities. Dollars and other ' hard currencies ' could be purchased in the so-called ' free ' markets that operated extensively in Switzerland and Egypt. Gold at upwards of $45 per ounce could be ' bought and sold, in the Middle East, India, Hong Kong, and European capitals '.[6] By 1950–51, when world confidence in sterling had again sharply depreciated, there was widespread evasion of exchange and other controls. At the beginning of that year the international free gold market was handling one million ounces per month. At the year's end it was dealing with four times that amount, and an estimated 2 billion dollars of ' free gold ' had changed hands.[7]

[1] Department of Interior (Australia), *Australia in Facts and Figures*, No. 26 (1950), p. 15.
[2] Association of British Chemical Manufacturers, *Report on the Chemical Industry* (1949), p. 58.
[3] ' Industrial Emigration,' *Scope*, June, 1951, pp. 76–80.
[4] For cement see the *Financial Times*, June 1, 1951. For Textiles see *Manchester Guardian*, April 5, 1951.
[5] T. Balogh, *Dollar Crisis : Causes and Cure* (1949)
[6] (South African) *Industrial Review*, February 1951, pp. 6–7.
[7] loc. cit. Who buys the gold,' the article asked. ' Hoarders in Europe as well as Asia.' The principal sellers, according to the *Industrial Review*, were South Africa and Southern Rhodesia, U.S.S.R., France and Belgium.

At the same time ' Sterling of many types [was] being bought and sold in a number of foreign centres ', chiefly in New York,[1] Belgium, and Italy.[2]

Still another type of capital export that developed under Labour was the wholesale migration to overseas areas of companies resident in the United Kingdom. The profits tax, it was noted frequently, gives ' added incentive to companies operating abroad to emigrate to the countries where they operate '.[3] In 1949–50 almost the entire copper-mining group of companies transferred control to either Northern or Southern Rhodesia,[4] and the *Financial Times* could claim that London had ' ceased to be the mining centre of the world '.[5] According to the British Overseas Mining Association, companies with a nominal capital of £40 million ' and with assets of many times that capital value . . . had emigrated to escape the onerous burden of the profits tax '.[6] Nor was the movement confined to mining companies. Among others, Anglo-Egyptian Oilfields departed for the freer enterprise of Cairo ; Anglo-American Telegraph found a haven in Southern Rhodesia ; and Sisal Estates departed for Kenya. Indeed it became necessary for some companies to issue statements to the effect that migration was not contemplated, against persistent rumours to that effect.[7] According to one observation made in 1949, in the preceding three years 202 public companies with an issued capital of over £80 million had either migrated to the Dominions or ' radically extended their manufacturing capacity there '.[8]

---

[1] An article in the *New York Times* (October 28, 1951) explained the mechanics of such transfers as follows : ' One wishes to transfer $1,000 to London and would rather remit £417 than the £347 one could send at the official rate. One goes to the foreign exchange dealer here and gives him a check. Two or three days later a, messenger arrives in the office of one's London connection and pays him sterling.

[2] *Manchester Guardian*, November 6, 1951.

[3] Oscar Hobson, City Editor, *News Chronicle*, April 11, 1951.

[4] Including the Nchanga Consolidated Copper Mines, Rhodesia Broken Hill Development, Rhodesia Copper Refineries, Rhokana Corporation, and Rhodesian Anglo-American Copper Mining Co. Following the move dividend payments increased 50 per cent.

[5] *Financial Times*, October 26, 1951.

[6] *Investors' Chronicle*, May 12, 1951.

[7] Lever Brothers and Unilever, Ltd., issued such a statement following a Reuter's report that the company was about to migrate to the United States. (*Financial Times*, May 31, 1951).

[8] ' Should Businesses Emigrate,' *Future*, Vol. 4, No. 2 (April–May, 1949), (continued on next page)

Toward the end of its term in office the Labour Government was forced to restrict the migration of companies to overseas areas. The Finance Act of 1951 contained a provision which made it illegal, without Treasury consent, to transfer overseas a company's seat of management and control, if it resulted, directly or indirectly, in the avoidance of liability for income tax or profits tax.

Migration was not, of course, a practical solution for most companies, nor was the export of capital possible for most wealthy individuals. Resistance therefore took the more conventional forms of pressure, persuasion, evasion and guerilla skirmishes between the Inland Revenue and privately-employed accountants. Certainly enormous exertions were made by the F.B.I., the National Union of Manufacturers, the Association of British Chambers of Commerce, the Institute of Directors and, of course, the Opposition, to convince the Government that on the one hand income tax was stifling initiative and frustrating production, while on the other profits tax was inhibiting industrial expansion and even preventing the replacement of assets. While it was not difficult to disprove most of these charges, there can be no doubt that the chorus of protest, in which nearly the entire press joined, served to make English people more conscious of their tax burdens than in any previous period—including the war. The importance of this campaign, although its immediate effects were not apparent, should not be underestimated. The climate of opinion which was then created will make it extremely difficult for any future Chancellor of the Exchequer to raise taxes even though the tax burden may fall lightly, or indeed not at all, on important sections of the community.

There can be no doubt that the problem of evasion was a serious one, and had been since the sharp increase in tax rates at the beginning of the war. It was estimated in 1949 that approxi-

The details were :

Country :				No. of firms	Issued Capital
Canada ...	...	...	...	40	10 million
Australia ...	...	...	...	129	50 ,,
New Zealand	...	...	...	8	3,300,000
South Africa	...	...	...	15	25 million
Southern Rhodesia		...	...	10	2 ,,

mately £100 million a year in taxes was beyond the reach of the tax collector, and that perhaps as many as 75,000 traders and merchants remained outside the tax net.[1] In 1951, in an effort to trace undeclared income the Labour Government went so far as to require the banks and certain other institutions to deliver to the Inland Revenue upon request the names of persons whose accounts were drawing interest beyond £15 annually. Subsequently 330,000 cases of under-assessment or non-assessment were revealed.[2]

In combating tax avoidance the Labour Government was confronted with considerable difficulties. Not the least of these was a shortage of tax collectors that was never fully remedied. In 1948-49, for example, the number of tax collectors was only 1,400 ' compared with 1,700 before the war and with a desirable completement of 2,000 '.[3]   A second important factor was the rôle of accountancy in post-war Britain.   Accountants themselves were loath to operate, in effect, as revenue agents. ' Our responsibility,' said a member of the Council of the Association of Certified and Corporate Accountants, ' to the outside world is definitely limited.' By reference to a famous decision in a leading tax case, he was able to illuminate the dilemma that accountants, presumably, will always face in the Welfare State. Lord Clyde, he pointed out, had made clear, by inference, the duty and function of accountants :

' No man in this country is under the smallest obligation, moral or other, so to arrange his legal relations to his business or to his property as to enable the Inland Revenue to put the largest possible shovel into his stores. The Inland Revenue is not slow—and quite rightly—to take every advantage which is open to it under the taxing statutes for the purpose of depleting the taxpayer's pocket. And the taxpayer is in like manner entitled to be astute to prevent,

[1] Douglas Houghton, M.P., in *Hansard*, Vol. 469, Cols. 1817-1828, November 14, 1949. Houghton was the secretary of the Inland Revenue Staff Federation.
[2] Report of the Comptroller and Auditor-General, *Revenue Departments Appropriation Accounts*, 1952-3.
[3] 1st, 2nd and 3rd Reports, Committee of Public Accounts, Session, 1948-49.

so far as he honestly can, the depletion of his means by the Revenue.'[1]

Lord Clyde's dictum, recalling the days when Spencer's *The Man Versus the State* was the Bible of Conservatives, and when it seemed a clear duty to resist each successive tax imposition on grounds of a conflict with higher laws of nature, is, of course, anachronistic in a society where the State, financed by taxation, is undertaking a vast responsibility for welfare and services.

As might be expected, one source of tax avoidance was the expense account. In the private business, of course, where there are few shareholders, the use of such accounts is limited only by what the Inland Revenue will tolerate, and in many cases expenses can be successfully concealed in administrative accounts. In the public company, in addition to the Revenue, shareholders are, theoretically, watch-dogs, but unless the shareholder is also an accountant he is unlikely to be able to distinguish—should he wish to do so—cost-of-living from cost-of-business expenses. For tax inspectors the task of distinguishing between genuine and spurious expenses is obviously extremely difficult. It requires the detailed examination of a large number of expense items, some legitimate, others not, which though petty in themselves may add up to substantial sums. From time to time sample investigations of expense allowances were conducted by the Inland Revenue. From one such investigation, involving the examination of 52 expense accounts, the Chief Inspector of Taxes reported

' The total expenses claimed were £127,896, and the amount agreed to be disallowed was £36,660—an average of £705 a case.'[2]

Another form of abuse which again benefited executives and directors in industry was the ' provision by the company of bene-

---

[1] C. A. Newport, ' The Accountant, the Client and the Revenue,' *Accountants Journal*, Vol. 43, No. 523 (September, 1951), p. 221. British accountants tend to identify their interest with those of industry generally, particularly in controversial matters such as taxation, controls, etc. See, for example, the Presidential Address of Lawrence W. Robson to the Institute of Cost and Works Accountants (June 1, 1951), reprinted in the *Accountant*, June 9, 1951, pp. 572–575.

[2] Sir Alfred Road, evidence submitted by the Inland Revenue to the *Royal Commission on the Taxation of Profits and Income*, July 8, 1954.

fits in kind, in the form of houses, services, cars, and things of that kind '.[1] While it is quite impossible to estimate the totals involved, it would not be unfair to say that much of the ' conspicuous living ' of the 1945–51 period was based on over-generous expense accounts and other forms of tax evasion.

The most important income component which escaped the tax net—and escaped it quite legitimately—was derived from capital gains. Since no capital gains tax was operated under the Labour Government, rises in share values and profits made from other kinds of capital transactions produced what amounted to tax-free income for recipients. Although the ordinary share index[2] rose rather slowly during the period—from 127 in 1945 (1938 = 100) to 155 in 1951—capital appreciation amounted to over £2,000 million, a tax-free gain distributed among Britain's 1¼ million shareholders and financial institutions. Dividend limitation was, of course, responsible for retarding share appreciation, but some rise was inevitable during a period of rapid industrial expansion, full employment and high profits.

The increase in the real value of company assets was reflected, particularly after 1949 when a small stamp duty was repealed, in the growing number of bonus issues that were made. While this practice provoked much criticism on the grounds that bonus shares provided an additional source of tax-free income, the riposte of company directors that bonus issues were simply book-keeping transactions designed to bring the nominal share capital of a business into line with its real value, was at least technically correct. Apart from some small advantage that might accrue from the enhanced marketability of shares, bonus issues in themselves added nothing to shareholders' incomes. The real objection to bonus issues, however, stemmed from the observed fact that they were generally, and contrary to Government policy, a prelude to increased dividend payments.[3] A company which

---

[1] E. R. Brooks, Commissioner of Inland Revenue, ibid.

[2] *London and Cambridge Economic Service* : Equity Share Index.

[3] See *Report of the Committee on Shares of No Par Value*, Cmd. 9112, March, 1954. The minority report of Mr. W. B. Beard contained a summary of a study made of the first 100 companies to make bonus issues after the duty was repealed in April, 1949. ' 62 of these 100 companies distributed more money (in some cases more than twice as much) in dividends in respect of the year following the bonus issue than in

(*continued on next page*)

did not wish to attract attention to increased disbursements was thus able by increasing its share capital to pay a larger dividend while declaring a lower dividend rate.[1] Higher dividends then resulted in share appreciation which in turn brought tax free gains to shareholders. ' Rights issues ' were, however, another matter since they frequently involved the sale of shares to existing stockholders at a figure below the ruling market price. In these cases, of course, capital profits immediately accrued.

It has already been noted that the Profits Tax discriminated sharply against distributed as opposed to undistributed profits. The policy of the Labour Government was to encourage company savings as a principal means of financing new investment. Between 1945 and 1951 very large reserves were in fact accumulated by companies, amounting to the enormous figure of over £5,500 million.[2] Although it is sometimes argued that undistributed profits are not income, a substantial portion of such profits constitute either the immediate or ultimate property of shareholders. As the Oxford economist, Mr. Dudley Seers pointed out, the

' growing pretence that undistributed profits are not anybody's income may be tactically advisable in the present economic situation, but it is of course not one which we need maintain in academic discussion. Undistributed profits are legally the income to the holders of the company's equity, i.e. the shareholders. Even though they are not immediately spendable they increase the company's financial strength, eventually affecting the value of the shares (whose rise is

respect of the preceding year, and this figure rose to 80 in the year but one following the bonus issue. Moreover, 41 of the 100 companies progressively increased their distribution in each of the two years following the bonus issue. The pattern for most of these companies was an increase in money dividends from one year to another accompanied by a reduction in percentage dividend. On the other hand, of 100 companies taken at random which did not issue bonus shares during the same period, comparable figures were 18 (compared with 62), 41 (compared with 80) and 6 (compared with 41) '.

[1] For example, a 10 per cent dividend paid on £1 million of share capital involves a dividend payment of £100,000. But if the capital is increased to £2 million, through a one-for-one bonus issue, a ' reduced ' 6 per cent dividend will result in a dividend payment of £120,000. In short, a larger dividend but at a lower dividend rate.

[2] *National Income and Expenditure Blue Book*, 1946–53. This figure is post-tax but before providing for depreciation and stock appreciation.

tax free), providing a fund out of which dividends can be maintained if earnings fall, and accruing to the ordinary shareholders when the company is wound up.'[1]

While dividend restraint had the effect of denying shareholders much of the immediate benefits of high profits, the Labour Government could not, of course, prevent eventual distribution. In the event, dividends have risen steeply since the fall of the Attlee administration. Estimates for 1954 indicate an increase in dividends of some 50 per cent over 1950, and the movement of the share index as a result reached record heights.

In view of these factors and in the absence of authoritative studies, it is difficult to measure accurately the success of the fair shares and income redistribution, policy of the Labour Government. While there can be no question that a signal advance was made, the extent of tax evasion and of capital gains must qualify the achievement. There is, however, as already noted, an inherent conflict or dilemma in a fair shares policy applied to a mixed economy. There must come a point on the road to equality where a further advance is no longer compatible with the continued existence of the private enterprise system. It can be argued that the Labour Government came in fact very near to this point.

The persistent policy of discriminating against shareholders, which reached its climax in the threatened statutory limitation of dividends in the summer of 1951, implicitly assumed both that the shareholder had no moral claim to his income and that, further, he was no longer performing a necessary role in the· economic system. Logically such assumptions can only lead to the extension of the public sector.

But if the private sector is not to be abolished, and in fact it was not the intention of the Labour Government to abolish it, then fair shares can never be carried so far as to deny the business man a ' satisfactory ' share of his profits, or to deny the investor an ' adequate ' return on his capital. If export markets are to be captured, if productivity is to be increased, if full employment is to be achieved, industry must be persuaded to expand its production and investors to risk their savings. There are practical limits,

---

[1] Dudley Seers, *The Levelling of Incomes Since 1938* (Oxford, 1950).

in other words, beyond which taxation cannot be extended. As a Labour Chancellor noted in April, 1951 : ' There are some who disapprove of profits in principle. I do not share their view. In an economy three-quarters of which is run by private enterprise, it is foolish to ignore the function of profit as an incentive.'[1] If, however, a fair shares policy is reduced in favour of fortuitous rewards for enterprise, the resultant compromise can rapidly become a threat to the stability of the Welfare State itself. The increase in profits and dividends may lead to a wage spiral, and both generate inflationary pressure. Trade unions become restive and demand an increase in the profits tax, a capital gains tax, or a capital levy.[2] In the face of these threats business groups become alarmed, and more capital may be exported or consumed. In short, the whole structure of the Welfare State comes under attack from both militant socialists and *laisser-faire* democrats. Pressed hard by these critics and by the underlying dilemma, the Labour Government in the autumn of 1951 was unable to find any solution ; and in fact the dilemma was resolved only by the General Election.

[1] Quoted in *The Times*, April 11, 1951.
[2] Nor were appeals from Labour Ministers for continued restraint successful. Mr. Gaitskell's attempt to reason away increases in prices, profits and dividends in his address to the T.U.C. in September, 1951, was, as *The Times* noted (September 5, 1951), ' heard in silence '. A month earlier H. G. Brotherton, President of the Confederation of Shipbuilding and Engineering Unions, had warned the Government that ' if prices and profits are going up, then so are wages. . . . Our colleagues on the political wing of the movement should also bear in mind that . . . restraint was exercised by the trade union movement, until the outrageous increase in profits and prices showed us to be the victims of an economic swindle. . . . We must state with the greatest emphasis that, irrespective of the nature of the government of the day, it is the task of the trade union movement to protect and advance the interests—and above all the economic interests—of its members.'
Presidential Address to the Annual Meeting (August 14, 1951), pp. 3–8.

CHAPTER VII

PUBLIC RELATIONS OF GOVERNMENT AND BUSINESS

' Let us only suffer any person to tell us his story, morning
and evening, but for one twelve-month, and he will become
our master.'   EDMUND BURKE.
' Three weeks of press work and the truth is acknowledged
by everyone.'   OSWALD SPENGLER.

It is generally thought that the British are a quiet people,
decorous in their public manners and possessing a modest awareness of their achievements. Like the principles of the British
Constitution, many of the values and motivations of British life
arise out of the traditions and customs of the society rather than
out of its conscious formulations. In America, on the other
hand, particularly in the last thirty years, there has been a tendency
to ' sell ' values and motivations as if they were commodities
essential to the national standard of living. Currently in the
U.S.A. many traditional principles are much less articles of faith
than of propaganda.

Yet to distinguish sharply the arts and science of American
public relations from their British counterpart is to over-state
present and future differences. Since 1949 in particular, British
business public relations experts have closely studied the American
experience, and have developed a number of similar methods and
techniques. Whether measured by expenditure, volume or
diversity of effort, British business relations is a conspicuous
example of the successful export of American enterprise and
know-how.

By contrast the public relations of the Labour Government
were inadequate and faulty in the extreme. It was one of the
anomalies of the period that while the role of Government
steadily increased and thus created innumerable new points of
contact and of friction between the citizen and the State, the
expenditure on Government information and public relation

services actually declined. The Central Office of Information, created in April, 1946 out of the war-time Ministry of Information as a ' professional and technical common service agency for all the Ministerial Departments ', started out in 1946–47 with a budget of £4,039,000. By 1951–52, the C.O.I. expenditure had been cut to £2,430,000—a reduction of 40 per cent in money terms and, allowing for inflation, of almost two-thirds in real terms.

This severe curtailment of the information services must in part be credited to the sustained campaign of criticism directed against the C.O.I. by the Opposition in Parliament and the press. It was alleged that the information services were costly and wasteful, a charge so powerfully pressed that in October, 1948, the Government set up an official committee under Sir Henry French ' to examine the cost of the Government home information services and to make recommendations as to any direction in which economies may be desirable or the organisation could be improved '.[1] The Committee's report, although generally indecisive, endorsed the popular clamour for economies, recommending that the Departments should cut down their 1949–50 expenditure which ' we regard as too high '.

Another, more serious, accusation that the information services were a mask for political propaganda, was directed particularly at the Departmental Public Relations Officers. ' The Government P.R.O. system', observed the *Daily Mail* on one occasion, ' is a direct menace to one of our fundamental freedoms.'[2] The *Daily Express*, which campaigned persistently for the total abolition of Government information services, argued that ' P.R.O.s become the propaganda agents for the Party in power and with the best of intentions could never be anything else '.[3] Similar charges were directed against Government films. On several occasions these were banned by cinema operators[4] on the grounds that ' some of the films used by the C.O.I. are tending to illustrate more and more the viewpoint of the Government in power '.[5]

[1] *Report of the Committee on the Cost of Home Information Services.* Cmd. 7836.
[2] *Daily Mail,* November 12, 1948.   [3] *Daily Express,* February 4, 1947.
[4] *Daily Mirror,* June 14, 1948.   [5] *Daily Graphic,* June 23, 1948.

In practice, these criticisms do not seem to have been justified. The conventions of English political life operate powerfully against the behaviour complained of. The Labour Government, as distinct from the Labour Party, could not and did not carry on explicit, direct Socialist propaganda. There was a clear distinction between Mr. Attlee as Prime Minister and Mr. Attlee as leader of the Labour Party, and between Messrs. Morrison, Bevan, Dalton and Shinwell as Ministers and the same gentlemen as members of the Labour Party Executive, and this distinction was reflected in the nature of Government information on the one hand, and of Party propaganda on the other. Certainly the tone of most C.O.I. publications was carefully neutral. So much so that the ' Budget and Your Pocket ' a typical explanatory leaflet could be described by Mr. Cyril Osborne, Conservative M.P., as ' such first-class Tory propaganda that I should urge every employer to order enough copies to give one to each of his workers '.[1] The verdict of *The Times* was one in which it is safe to say most Englishmen would concur : ' Propaganda through Departmental channels of publicity is not a main charge that can be fairly brought against the Government.'[2]

Although the Government was debarred from making Socialist propaganda, it had a clear duty to use its information and propaganda services to help carry out the programme which had been placed before the electorate. The basic criticism of the Government public relations is, therefore, not that it failed to show how its programme related to Socialism, but that it failed to show with sufficient clarity and force how its programme related to immediate and long-term British problems and needs. In part, as we shall see, this failure can be ascribed to faulty techniques ; still more to inadequate expenditures. But the root cause must be traced to the failure of the Labour Government at the highest level to appreciate the role that public information and education services must play in the successful execution of democratic Socialist policy.

This failure is the more surprising since the Labour Government's conception of planning as expressed theoretically in the

---

[1] *Daily Telegraph*, May 28, 1949.
[2] *The Times*, May 14, 1948.

1947 *Economic Survey* and in numerous Ministerial statements, and administratively in the system of consultation and quasi-control, implicitly assumes a major role for co-operation between ' Government, industry and the people '. Moreover, in the uncontrolled and semi-controlled areas of the economy, persuasion was the principal means the Government possessed of influencing events. Mass advertising, for example, was essential to attract enough entrants to under-manned industries. Similarly—to mention only a few of the purposes of Government propaganda—it was necessary to launch campaigns for such diverse purposes as national savings, fuel economy, immunisation of children, road safety, and recruitment to the regular forces.

In addition to these ' action campaigns ', the information services had to relay the many aspects of Government policy which directly affected the citizen. Food rationing, the National Health Service and the complex system of National Insurance, all of which affected the entire population, necessitated on a vast scale a continuous stream of explanatory information.

But perhaps the most important and difficult of all the C.O.I.'s tasks were the economic information campaigns through which the Government was ' to take the people frankly into its confidence, however difficult the position of the country may be ' and to explain 'what has to be done to rebuild our economy on firm foundations '.[1] When a Government assumes, as the Labour Government assumed, direct responsibility for overall economic policy and social welfare, such campaigns are indeed essential. Labour had to explain, amongst other things, why wage restraint was necessary; why factory building was important at a time when a great housing shortage existed ; why goods urgently needed in the home market had to be exported ; and why production and productivity had become of crucial importance while memories of pre-war over-production were still fresh.

It was not until April, 1947, almost two years after the Labour Government took office, that an intensive educational and information effort was begun. There was widespread evidence that the *Economic Survey for* 1947 (Cmd. 7046) had not been given popular reception, and Sir Stafford Cripps, Chancellor of the

[1] *Economic Survey for* 1947. Cmd. 7046.

Exchequer, announced that the Government would undertake a strenuous campaign to acquaint the public with the facts set forth in the *Survey*.

To help carry out the campaign, a small Economic Information Unit was established within the Treasury to work with the Economic Planning Staff and the C.O.I. The Information Unit was charged with the preparation of a new ' Fortnightly Report to the Nation ', and semi-monthly press conferences were held by the leading Ministers concerned with economic affairs. Posters, press advertising, charts and diagrams were all extensively used and as a major effort a popular version of the *Economic Survey for 1947* was produced under the title of ' Battle for Output '. This achieved a sale of nearly 200,000 copies, an encouraging omen. The following year the peak of the information campaign was reached. The popular version of the 1948 *Economic Survey* sold nearly 440,000 copies, ' almost certainly a record for a publication of such a kind and on such a subject '.[1] In 1949, the campaign and the expenditure began to tail off : the three main publications, ' Survey 1949 ', ' The Budget and Your Pocket ', and ' Getting On Together ', achieved a total of just over half-a-million sales.

Taken at face value, the information campaigns of 1947–49 reached substantial proportions. Yet the evidence seems to show that the large-scale use of posters, films, lectures and other media failed to communicate the desired information. An analysis of some of the material presented to the public reveals, as one important cause of the failure, that much of the language and terminology employed was badly chosen for popular communication. There is clear evidence that a majority of the *interested* public, itself a minority of the total adult population, was unable to understand and assimilate much of what it read or heard discussed with regard to the economic situation.

According to a careful study by Mass-Observation[2] ' The Battle for Output ', the popular version of Cmd. 7046, was ' incapable of directly influencing most of the population to any significant degree. This majority includes millions of sensible and intelligent citizens in responsible production jobs '. The M-O

[1] Central Office of Information : Annual Report 1947–48. Cmd. 7567.
[2] *The Language of Leadership*, March 20, 1947.

survey showed that words and phrases frequently used in the White Paper, e.g. ' ultimately ', ' resources ', ' subordinates ', ' formulate ', ' conception ', ' rigid application ', were often misunderstood or not understood at all. The sentence, ' The gap between resources and requirements will in the end be closed by some of the requirements being left unsupplied ', M-O reported, ' positively infuriated some, who didn't think it made sense at all. Most could make little of it '. The concluding sentence in the White Paper, ' The OBJECTIVES of this Paper EMBODY the Government's determination to put first things first ', created, according to M-O, ' semi-paralysis '; while 'A democratic Government must therefore conduct its economic planning in a manner which preserves the maximum possible freedom of choice to the individual citizen ', was ' typically ' misinterpreted to mean :

' I should imagine the Government wants the working-class people to get every benefit that's going.'
' Government should be all out for the working classes.'
' It's to get the choice of people to get to know whether they're doing right or wrong.'
' I think it is saying that we're *not* going to have freedom of choice.'
' Can't make head or tail of it.'

The evidence of the M-O that the popular publications failed to communicate appears to be substantiated by the findings of the *Social Survey*, an organ of the C.O.I., which carried out a monthly survey in 1948 to determine the extent to which the public had become aware of the nation's outstanding problems. These findings must have made depressing reading for the campaign's sponsors. During a period of considerable economic stress in which a major crisis was held at bay only by the monthly arrival of Marshall Aid, 49 per cent of respondents thought ' Things are going well for Britain on the whole ', as against 28 per cent who thought things were going badly, and 23 per cent who had no opinion. From replies to more specific questions it was abundantly clear that the whole emphasis of the 1947 and 1948 *Economic Surveys* had not been grasped.

These findings can be used to argue, of course, that the problem of mass communication is inherently insoluble. The argument, as advanced by Walter Lippmann and others, assumes that in modern society the average citizen cannot experience the facts at first hand, and cannot gain an adequate knowledge of them through communication. The conclusion appears to follow that political leadership must be confined to an informed, fact-conscious *élite* who will make intelligent decisions.

The argument is persuasive, and seemingly supported by the Labour Government experience, but several objections must be noted. In the first place, communication of ideas by British business was somewhat more expert and effective, as will be demonstrated, and this would suggest that the Government's failure was partially, at least, a technical one. Secondly, the Labour Government never attempted economic education on the requisite scale. As the 1947–48 C.O.I. annual report ruefully complained, ' The full expenditure on Government advertising at present levels . . . falls outstandingly short of that (of private advertising) on toilet and beauty preparations alone '. Moreover, there is clearly a twilight area in communications where knowledge can be compressed or shortened but not falsified or distorted. As M-O itself concludes :

> Ordinary people are interested in and concerned about serious issues. But most can only think and talk in their own version of our language. For ordinary PROPAGANDA (and politics) complete intelligibility is not necessarily essential—and may even be undesirable—since to a large degree emotional factors and considerations, of 'social prestige' operate. But in matters of INFORMATION where it is imperative that the whole public should understand facts—that is, should react *logically*—language becomes a primary consideration. To talk to everyone is not, as so many specialists suppose, to talk down. Popularisation is not to be confused (as it incessantly is confused) with Vulgarisation. The White Paper would have lost nothing by being written more directly ; the effect could have been enormously greater.

The actual sales figures of the popular versions of the 1947 and 1948 *Economic Surveys* revealed a widespread eagerness for economic information, which, had retrenchment been avoided, might have greatly helped the Government in the crisis days of 1949 and 1951. Yet it was precisely these economic information campaigns which the French Committee had singled out for criticism. Acknowledging that there had been some improvement in general understanding of basic economic facts, the Committee nevertheless urged that

> ' for the future still greater reliance should be placed on Ministerial speeches and press conferences, on the provision of information and material for discussion, and on helping interested groups to educate their own members. We think it should then be possible to achieve a marked decrease in the expenditure on paid publicity for the economic information campaign and we are glad to be informed in evidence that a contraction of expenditure on these lines is actually contemplated.'

Since expenditure on economic information—as distinct from other C.O.I. campaigns—never exceeded £600,000 in any year, the Government's acceptance of the Committee's recommendation must have reflected either disillusionment with the earlier campaigns or complacency with the temporarily improved economic situation. At any rate, it was decided both that recruitment for under-manned industries had become less urgent and that the crucial problems of 1949–50—balance of payments, low level of reserves, dangers of inflation—were ' themes for which press and poster advertising were not the easiest media to use, and in the summer of 1949 they ceased. . .".[1]

So the official information campaigns petered out. Unfortunately for the Attlee Government, the various non-official organisations which supported the Labour cause either could not or did not fill the gap that was left. In the press the balance of advantage was tipped heavily in favour of the Conservatives. Of the 12 national morning and evening newspapers in 1946–47 with a total circulation of almost 19 million, only 2, with a circulation of 5,900,000 were reliably committed to the Government's support.

[1] Central Office of Information : Annual Report, 1949–50. Cmd. 8081.

Although ' the power of the Tory Press ' and Labour counter-measures was a recurring theme at Labour Party conferences, no major new publication was launched in the whole period either by the Party, the trade unions, or the Co-operative Union. Funds spent on propaganda, publicity and political education seem in retrospect to be derisorily small. Thus in the critical inter-election year, 1950–51, after the February 1950 general election had shown a Conservative gain of 3 million votes, the Labour Party spent £57,000 on Party literature (including pamphlets, magazines, leaflets and posters), the T.U.C. less than £14,000 on ' printing, publishing and stationery ', and the Co-operative Union, £23,000. The expenditure of the Fabian Society should also be included, but the sums involved were tiny, partly because the Society had never attempted to influence opinion outside the intelligentsia. Individual unions spent additional sums, most of which were swallowed up in the publication of monthly journals—seldom read and often of poor quality.

Thus no co-ordinated propaganda or educational campaign was attempted by the Labour Movement. It is not surprising, therefore, that neither the Labour Government, the Labour Party nor their affiliates, were able to ' produce informed public opinion on which the success of a new social system ultimately depends '.[1] Throughout the period 1945–51, despite frequent warnings of failure and demands for improvement of Party publicity and propaganda, little effective action was taken. Indeed, because the failure of public relations was clearly antici-pated, in the event it was all the more remarkable. Although, admittedly, it was difficult to dramatise the personnel and policies of the Labour Government, particularly in a period of post-war emotional slump, there was no intensive or expert attempt to do so. At the same time, as expected, many of the Government's measures were

> of a character to arouse strong opposition among particular groups or possessing interests who will employ all the means they can to convince public opinion that these measures are wrong and should be opposed.[2]

[1] T. Balogh, *The Dollar Crisis : Causes and Cure* (Oxford, 1949), p. 95.
[2] Francis Williams, *Press, Parliament and People.* London, 1946. p. 129.

'Strong opposition' was aroused and the means used by British business to advance its point of view were with few exceptions slick, varied and effective. Propaganda was devoted not merely to short-term objectives, such as changes in specific policies of the Labour Government, but also to long-term business goals, such as the popularisation of free enterprise. While it is difficult to estimate the efficacy of the various campaigns and efforts, it can be suggested that the total effect had important political consequences, particularly in influencing the attitudes and outlooks that crystallize as public and political opinion.[1] By 1950–51 Labour Party circles were aware that British industry's public relations activities were a considerable threat to the Party's objectives,[2] and on March 7, 1951, the industrialist who had led the campaign against sugar nationalisation, noting that nationalisation of sugar had not been included in the King's Speech opening Parliament, could boast that ' we have . . . won the first round '.[3]

It was not until early 1948, however, that industry began an organised effort to influence public opinion. Thus far nationalisation had been acceptable to important elements in industry and, as has been noted, controls had not been operated at the expense of business self-government. Taxation was then below the wartime level, and full employment had resulted in, among other things, the maximisation of profits. Privately, at least, many industralists were of the opinion that the Labour Government had proved far more co-operative than had been expected.

At the Scarborough Labour Party Conference in May, 1948, delegates were assured that a bill to nationalise iron and steel would be introduced during the current Parliament, following

---

[1] As noted by Leo Bogart of the New Jersey Standard Oil Public Relations Department : ' The effect of the [institutional advertising] messages is not expressed in action but is lodged in the minds of the reading or listening public. Presumably it takes the form of a changed set of attitudes, a more favourable set of associations to the name of a particular institution or industry.' ' Use of Opinion Research,' *Harvard Business Review*, March, 1951, p. 119.

[2] See, for example, ' Capitalist Propaganda is Licking Us ', *The Railway Review*, January 19, 1951 ; Peter Shore, ' Big Business Invades Politics ', *Socialist Commentary*, January, 1952, pp. 14–17 ; John Cates, ' The Politics of Free Enterprise ', *The New Statesman and Nation*, January 12, 1952, pp. 31–32.

[3] Lord Lyle at the 48th Annual General Meeting of Tate and Lyle, Ltd., reported in the *Economist*, March 10, 1951, pp. 22–23.

press reports that the action had been indefinitely postponed; and Herbert Morrison, in a statement on behalf of the Party Executive, announced that ' in the next programme it will fight —and I can promise you that the Executive will do it— to give proper consideration to further propositions for public ownership '.[1]   In April, 1949, the Labour Party Policy Statement proposed for nationalisation industrial life assurance, sugar, cement, meat wholesaling and slaughtering, water, and ' all suitable minerals '.[2]

The reaction of industries concerned was immediate.   The meat, cement, and sugar industries, among others, hired a public relations firm to organise campaigns against nationalisation in particular, and bulk-buying, municipal trading, controls and taxation in general.   The insurance, iron and steel, and textiles industries undertook similar campaigns through their own public relations organisations.   A number of trade associations appointed special public relations or press officers, and there was a significant increase in institutional advertising in the press.   Finally, in December, 1948, at the Federation of British Industries Conference on Publicity, considerable attention was paid to the whole question of ' the publication of information about industry as *news* in the editorial columns of the press ', as distinct from advertising.   ' We in industry ', said F.B.I. Director Sir Frederick Bain, ' have been slack, I think, in not getting over the simple, plain facts.   If that is the purpose of publicity, then the sooner we get down to thinking seriously about how to put the matter right, the better '.[3]

In the years that followed, much of the publicity and public relations was explicitly patterned after American experience. British subsidiaries of American advertising agencies lent inspiration and ideas to the various efforts,[4] and the American Advertising Council helped organise campaigns similar to the ' sell business to America ' type it carried on in the United States.[5]   Stock

---

[1] *Report of the 47th Annual Conference of the Labour Party*, May, 1948, p. 122.

[2] Labour Party, *Labour Believes in Britain*, April, 1949.

[3] F.B.I., *News of Industry* (August, 1949), p. 1.

[4] For example, publicity and public relations for the London Stock Exchange is handled by the London offices of the J. Walter Thompson advertising agency.

[5] The phrase is that of Robert M. Gray, advertising and sales promotion manager

(*continued on next page*)

splitting, as a device for increasing ownership and interest in industry was encouraged on the grounds that it had demonstrated its value in America,[1] and companies were urged to Americanise the presentation of their accounts and reports.[2] The public relations campaign of the London Stock Exchange incorporated techniques followed by the New York Stock Exchange,[3] and large-scale business support of educational and other institutions drew encouragement from American practice.[4]

Indeed, in general, as Mr. Wincott, the editor of the *Investors' Chronicle*, noted,

> the United States has a great deal to teach us here. Exactly how much can really only be appreciated if you have actually experienced the completely contrasting commercial climates of the two countries. . . . To convince the British public that, for example, high profits honestly earned are a reason for rejoicing among the workers; to persuade workers that it is in their interest to help get rid of inefficiency and restraint of trade ; to demonstrate to them that the opportunities for personal advancement are at their maximum under free enterprise—to do all this and a great deal more of a general educational character is going to require vast stores of faith,

of Esso Standard Oil and co-ordinator of the Council's ' campaign to publicise the American economic system '. *New York Times*, February 10, 1952. According to the *Times* story, ' as a direct result of the (Council's) programme similar campaigns were started with the Council's aid in England and Australia.'

[1] ' Lex,' columnist for the *Financial Times*, noted that ' we have frequently had evidence from the United States of the value of share splitting as a means of spreading interest more widely among investors . . .' June 1, 1951.

[2] The *Accountant*, February 24, 1951, p. 177, arguing for greater disclosure of information in company accounts, pointed out that American companies ' realise the propaganda value implicit in such disclosures '.

[3] On July 17, 1951, the *Financial Times* stated that 'An American idea which deserves consideration for application in this country is the dissemination to listed companies by the New York Stock Exchange of propaganda by companies designed to " encourage a wider knowledge of the risks and benefits of stock ownership and the function of the stockholder " . . . The Americans are more fortunate than we are. They have not yet had a severe dose of nationalisation. Whether they are more far-sighted is a moot point. Perhaps they are being forewarned by our experience. The urgency of the task compels admiration for a method which uses many hands and many channels—and distributes the burden of cost '. The London Stock Exchange subsequently undertook to distribute the information described.

[4] The *Financial Times* and other business journals published numerous accounts of American industry-sponsored research foundations, institutes, university courses, teaching and fellowship programmes, etc. See, for example, ' Taxation Tactics in U.S.A. ', *Financial Times*, August 30, 1951.

courage, imagination and drive, as well as not a little money. We can comfort ourselves, however, with the knowledge that America has proved that it can be done. And already in this country various interests have made a start. It is always difficult to measure the effects of an educational campaign. But there is no reason to doubt that the vigorous efforts of some of the erstwhile candidates for nationalisation, those wicked animals who have the temerity to defend themselves when attacked, have borne good fruit.[1]

Of the erstwhile candidates to which Mr. Wincott referred, Tate and Lyle, Britain's largest sugar refiners, were outstanding in the vigour and skill with which they organised their anti-nationalisation campaign. Employing Aims of Industry, a public relations firm founded to promote business interests, Tate and Lyle demonstrated what could be achieved by industry propaganda. Mr. Cube, a cartoon-style figure sugar lump proclaiming anti-nationalisation slogans, appeared each day on more than two million sugar packages, on 100,000 ration book holders distributed free to housewives by Tate and Lyle, and on all Tate and Lyle delivery trucks. Propaganda was inserted into material on the sugar refining industry sent out to 4,500 schools. Six mobile film vans toured the entire United Kingdom, and more than 3,000 speeches or lectures were delivered to factory and working men's clubs, youth and university organisations, women's clubs, schools, and even groups of soldiers in His Majesty's Forces. Stories or news items concerned with sugar and sponsored by Aims filled 15,000 column inches in 400 newspapers, approximately £200,000 worth of space. According to Tate and Lyle's own estimates, in a period of two years, 1948–50, their total advertising, including the campaign, cost more than £240,000, or 240 per cent as much as Tate and Lyle spent on advertising in 1947–48.[2]

In addition to the general publicity campaign, an effort was made to enlist the support of labour for anti-nationalisation. In early 1949 a telegram described by Aims as ' historic ' was sent

[1] Harold Wincott in the *Financial Times*, October 23, 1951.
[2] *Financial Times*, May 31, 1951.

to Mr. W. A. Bustamente, head of the Jamaican Industrial Trades Union, requesting amplification—for syndication to British newspapers—of critical comments on sugar nationalisation which Bustamente had been reported to have made.

Bustamente's reply was subsequently featured in whole or in part in more than 100 newspapers, without, however, any indication that it had been solicited. After stating that nationalisation would drive foreign investors out of Jamaica, thereby creating unemployment and further weakening Jamaica's economic position, he continued,

> We over here have enough experience of your nationalisation over there. We do not want it ; we do not intend to have it.
> . . .
> I, of course, believe in private enterprise and realise one fact that nationalisation does not lead to the road to success or prosperity, but destruction of a country and its people of all classes.

A later statement from Bustamente threated a general strike in Jamaica if sugar were nationalised.

Attention was also paid to the labour side on the home front. Richard Dimbleby, a popular B.B.C. commentator, was hired to make an extensive recording of interviews with contented Tate and Lyle employees. He visited the principal refineries, and eventually some 400 albums of six records each were used by Aims for various purposes. In September, 1950, a profit-sharing agreement was negotiated by Tate and Lyle with the National Union of General and Municipal Workers, representing Tate and Lyle employees. The agreement served to support the contention that labour relations at Tate and Lyle could hardly be improved by nationalisation which, of course, would destroy the profit-sharing scheme.

It is difficult to measure the results of the Tate and Lyle-Aims campaign against sugar nationalisation. Certainly it is impossible to assess its influence on the votes cast in the 1950 Election. But aside from tributes to its effectiveness paid by both the *Financial Times* and the *Economist*, it is at least significant that a poll taken by the British Institute of Public Opinion in November, 1950, showed that 57 per cent of those questioned were opposed to sugar nationalisation, while only 25 per cent approved.[1]

Since Labour's share of the total votes in both the 1950 and 1951 elections was approximately 48 per cent, it is clear that a very large number of Labour supporters were not convinced by the Party's case for nationalisation. This was bound to influence Party policy and it was a feature of both the 1951 election manifesto and the 1953 policy statement *Challenge to Britain* that no official mention of the sugar refining industry was made. Labour circles in Britain were of the opinion that Tate and Lyle had had the better of the nationalisation argument.

But perhaps the chief significance of the Tate and Lyle campaign was that it launched Aims into large-scale public relations on behalf of British industry, and at the same time encouraged similar campaigns by other industry-related organisations. By 1950 Aims was supported by more than 2,000 business firms, and its Board of Directors included Lord Perry of the (British) Ford and Firestone companies, Sir George Nelson of English Electric, Sidney Bruce Askew of Rank's flour mills, George F. Earle of the Associated Portland Cement group, Sir George Usher of Aberdare Cables, Garfield Weston of Allied Bakeries, and J. Arthur Rank of the Rank Organisation. It had been officially recommended to British industry by the F.B.I., and its annual operating budget was in the neighbourhood of £100,000. It had handled campaigns for, among others, the meat, wholesale textile, chemicals, cement, boot and shoe, iron and steel, rum, flour milling, baking, building, sugar, petroleum and tobacco industries, and, further, had maintained a ' sustained attack ' on ' bulk-buying, municipal trading, nationalisation, unnecessary controls, purchase tax, and bureaucracy '. In 1950 it placed 93,983 column inches of propaganda in some 497 newspapers, worth almost £2 million at advertising rates. In 1948–49 it provided ' speakers, facilities, contacts, scripts and ideas for a total of 63 broadcasts in industrial and allied subjects in the Home and Light programmes ' of the B.B.C. Its film bureau in 1951 had served more than two million people since October, 1949, and it had prepared 85 extensive

[1] H. H. Wilson. '*Techniques of Pressure—Anti-Nationalisation Propaganda in Britain,*' *Public Opinion Quarterly*, Summer, 1951, pp. 225–242.

speakers' briefs on a wide variety of subjects, and established a 200-man speakers' bureau. It had also organised a Parliamentary Relations Division which ' supplies Members of Parliament of any Party with facts about Industry. It also takes necessary Parliamentary action to assist Industry's case in both Houses. Where advisable it promotes questions in the House '.

With the exception of press advertising, which was extensively used by other organisations, many of the techniques developed by Aims in the sugar campaign were subsequently applied to a number of public relations efforts. The Cement Marketing Federation inscribed anti-cement nationalisation slogans on every bag of cement and on every cement truck. Insurance salesmen carried insurance propaganda into homes when they came to collect premiums, and associations of insurance companies extensively advertised the merits of ' Free Enterprise Insurance ' in the press.[1] The Wholesale Textile Association, through a publicity campaign financed by a levy on its members, undertook to educate the public in the functions of the wholesaler. During 1951 it planned to allocate approximately £10,000 to press advertising, booklets and brochures designed to reach trade people and ordinary citizens.[2]

The London Stock Exchange undertook a separate campaign incorporating, in the words of the *Investors' Chronicle*, 'the adoption of modern publicity methods aimed at educating the public about the investment facts of life '.[3] Numerous articles describing the functions of the Exchange appeared in the national press,[4] and a special booklet, *The Stock Exchange : Some Questions and Answers* was published and widely distributed by the Stock Exchange Council.[5]

[1] Insurance advertising increased from an expenditure of £93,000 (round figures) in the last six months of 1948, to £294,700 in 1949, to £357,000 in 1950, to £198,800 in the first six months of 1951. Of these amounts, the Industrial Life Offices Association, which handled a portion of the industry's institutional advertising, spent £49,500 in September–November, 1949 ; £78,600 in 1950 ; and £42,900 in the first six months of 1951. (Compiled from the *Statistical Review of Press Advertising*, London, 1951).

[2] Hazel Kitson, ' Explaining the Wholesaler ', *Scope : Magazine for Industry*, September, 1951. [3] *Investors' Chronicle*, April 21, 1951.

[4] See, for example, Lord Catto, ' In Defence of the City ', *Sunday Times*, September 9, 1951.

[5] The booklet begins : ' The Stock Exchange is the market where stocks and

(*continued on next page*)

Public relations efforts of individual British industries were supplemented by efforts carried on by industry and trade-wide organisations. The Economic League, founded in 1919 and financed by industry, considerably increased its activities. The League, which is concerned primarily with working-class opinion, exists

> to promote and improve the knowledge and study of economics and of other industrial and social subjects affecting the interests of the community and of members thereof, from the standpoint that—(1) The preservation of personal freedom and free enterprise is essential to national well-being, (2) While maintaining its complete independence of any political party the League must actively oppose all subversive forces —whatever their origin or inspiration—that seek to undermine the security of Britain in general and British industry in particular.[1]

In 1950 it employed 100 speakers and distributors of literature, 53 of whom were employed full-time—'men and women who understand the point of view of the man at the bench or the woman on the loom, because they have themselves, worked in mines, docks, or factories . . . [and] who speak not only to an audience they know but in an accent and in an idiom that is homely and familiar '.[2] During 1950 the League held over 19,000 meetings, distributed 18,000,000 leaflets, and obtained more than 30,000 column inches of press publicity. Leaflet subjects included : Insurance, Risk in Free Enterprise, Iron and Steel, Menace of Communism, Profits, Savings, Taxation, Nationalisation, and the Sheffield ' Peace Congress '.[3] Wherever possible, the League enlists employers to distribute leaflets in the pay packets of workers, and it holds meetings and group talks on company time. It also appraises employers of sentiment and opinion among workers.

Of the organisations similar in purpose to Aims of Industry

---

shares are bought and sold in the quickest, cheapest and fairest manner ' (p. 3) and goes on to make many debatable assertions, e.g. ' But the fact is that the Stock Exchange is quite powerless to influence the major trends of prices.' (p. 6).

[1] Economic League, 31*st Annual Report* (1950), p. 3.
[2] Hazel Kitson, ' The Economic League ', *Persuasion*, June, 1950, p. 4 (reprint).
[3] Economic League, op. cit., p. 5.

and the Economic League, the Council of Retail Distributors is one of the most interesting. Formed in 1947, the Council is unique in that all of its presidents, David Gammans, Ernest Maples, and Major Guy Lloyd, have been Conservative M.P.s. Of its 27 vice-presidents in 1950, 18 were also Conservative M.P.s. Describing itself as ' guided by no other interest than that of the private trader ', the Council promotes Parliamentary action on matters concerning industry, and carries on a number of services for its members including research, publicity and advice. It opposes nationalisation, State trading, high taxation and ' unnecessary ' controls. At its Annual Conference in April, 1950, the Council's Director-General, Lionel Fowler, declared that the Council's policy was ' concentration on plenty of printed matter and propaganda as the main objective, [with] the monthly journal and individual recruitment second '.[1]

In July, 1951, the influential and fast-growing Institute of Directors, whose 4,500 members[2] comprise the top echelon in British industry management, announced that it was launching a Free Enterprise Campaign on the occasion of ' the entry of the Welfare State into its seventh year '. The Campaign, it explained

> ' came into being following talks with a number of organisations with similar interests including the Federation of British Industries, the National Union of Manufacturers, the Association of British Chambers of Commerce and the National Chamber of Trade.'[3]

The Campaign, the cost of which was unofficially estimated at £200,000 during the first year of operation,[4] mainly involves press advertising aimed at youth and stressing ' as the most telling points for free enterprise the *choice* which it gives the consumer and the *chance* which it gives the employee to get on '. The Campaign will probably be criticised, it was stated in the Institute of Directors' publication, *The Director*,

> ' on the grounds that it is political propaganda. In so far as nationalisation is a political issue, then the campaign by

[1] Council of Retail Distributors, *Enterprise and Traders' Digest*, Vol. 4 No. 2 (Spring 1950), pp. 204–205.
[2] Over 10,000 by December, 1954.
[3] *The Director*, Vol. 2, No. 9 (July, 1951) p. 50.
[4] *Evening Standard*, July 26, 1951.

stating the case for free enterprise is political. But, and this cannot be too strongly emphasised, there is a sharp dividing line between politics and party politics, and the Free Enterprise Campaign, which is being paid for by industry and commerce, is not " inspired by, nor has any direct or indirect connection with any political party ".'[1]

The disclaimer of party politics by the Institute of Directors followed the general pattern of British industry public relations. Neither Aims of Industry, the Economic League nor other organisations admit political or party orientation. Their disavowal of public relations politics has been challenged, however, not merely by Labour Party supporters but by elements in industry itself. The expression, ' Of course this isn't being political ', *Commercial Motor* noted in November, 1949

' [is] much used in transport circles of late, particularly when the conversation has turned to the future of the industry, or to nationalisation. Any sentiment likely to gladden the heart of one or other of the political leaders is hastily followed by a deceptively frank avowal of political disinterestedness. It is as much a ritual as throwing spilt salt over the left shoulder.'

Commenting on the Free Enterprise Campaign, the business journal *Scope* predicted that the Campaign's disclaimer of party politics would evoke ' coarse belly laughter from politicians.'

' What do the Institute of Directors want the receiver of their advertising message to *do* after being convinced that free enterprise is a system conspicuously to his advantage ? There is only one possible answer. They want him to vote Conservative.'[2]

While there can be little doubt that this was the essential purpose of all the industry publicity campaigns, there were important practical reasons why the political motive should be denied. Since the period of the First World War, when memories of the political interventions of the Free Trade Union and the Tariff

---

[1] *The Director.*
[2] *Scope*, September, 1951, pp. 92–93.

Reform League were green, English electoral law had contained provisions which sought to exclude monied interests from the electoral struggle. Section 34 of the 1918 Representation of the People Act read

> 'A person other than the election agent of a candidate shall not incur any expense on account of holding public meetings or issuing advertisements, circulars or publications for the purpose of promoting the election of a candidate . . . unless he is authorised in writing to do so. . . .'

Since each candidate was restricted by the same law to a relatively modest campaign expenditure, the purpose of the Act was both to channel all outlays through the established political parties and at the same time to impose a ceiling on electoral expenditures so that great wealth should not unduly influence public opinion. In 1949, the Labour Government's Representation of the People Act appeared to re-state, in somewhat different words, the relevant sections of the 1918 Act.

The question which arose in 1950 and again in 1951 was whether the various publicity campaigns, if continued during the period of a General Election, would infringe the election law. Warnings in late 1949 and early 1950 were directed at ' Mr. Cube ' by both Sir Hartley Shawcross, the Attorney-General, and Mr. Herbert Morrison. Although the law had not been tested in the Courts, it was generally believed that it would prohibit such expenditures, and it was noticeable that after the 1950 Election date had been announced, and until the poll had been counted, the activities of Aims of Industry and the Economic League were suspended as far as they could be. No case, therefore, arose out of the 1950 Election. But in 1951, what seemed to be a very flagrant breach of the electoral law took place. In the middle of the October E'ection campaign, the Tronoh-Malayan Tin Group of Companies caused an advertisement to appear in *The Times* which, it was submitted, was ' a plain invitation to readers to vote anti-Socialist on October 25th. . . . Readers of the advertisement could not have been told to vote Conservative more plainly if those words had been actually used '.[1]

---

[1] *Manchester Guardian,* February 15, 1952. Mr. Christmas Humphreys, senior Treasury counsel at the Old Bailey.

The ensuing prosecution, undertaken by the Crown, failed. Although it is by no means certain that the wording of the 1918 Act would have sufficed, the changes in the 1949 Act created unforeseen difficulties for the prosecution. For in place of the earlier relatively simple exclusion of unauthorised expenditure on behalf of a candidate, section 63 of the 1949 Act had imported a form of words which was interpreted to forbid only those expenditures which actually ' presented to the electors the candidate or his views.'

This, of course, the Tronoh advertisement, which was largely an attack on the Labour Government's proposals for dividend limitation, did not do. In what was acknowledged to be a test case the Judge summed up

' I accept the submission that section 63 does not prohibit expenditure the real purpose and effect of which is general and political propaganda, even though that general political propaganda does incidentally assist a particular candidate against others.[1]

The implications of this verdict are important, for it would seem to legitimise all propaganda expenditure, however massive, during election campaigns, providing that the propaganda is not directed to secure the return of *individual* candidates. This prohibition of support for individual candidates is, however, virtually valueless as a safeguard since modern electioneering in Britain pays little attention to personalities and to local affairs and is almost wholly concerned with broad national issues.

As Mr. Christmas Humphreys in his closing speech for the Crown said

' Enormous placards and advertisements can be put all over a constituency at unlimited cost stating : Vote Conservative and turn out the Socialists.'

The uneasiness with which some Labour supporters now regard the possible effects of business intervention in future

[1] *The Times*, February 19, 1952.

elections has been intensified by another legal decision which has removed a further obstacle to business expenditure on politics. The case arose out of the heavy outlay of Tate and Lyle in their anti-nationalisation campaign. The Company maintained that these expenditures were ' solely and exclusively laid out for the purpose of the trade ' and consequently should be treated as advertising expenses entitling the company to substantial tax reliefs. This claim was resisted by the Inland Revenue which argued that the purpose of the campaign was not to maintain the profits and goodwill of the Company—an accepted purpose of advertising—but only to decide who should earn them. After successive appeals, the House of Lords in July 1954 decided in favour of the Company. Nationalisation, it was held, would have resulted in the acquisition of the assets of the company and the Directors were entitled to the view that this would have effected the company's ability to maintain its profits and goodwill. Therefore, Tate and Lyle's advertising expenditure was allowable under the tax laws. At the same time, however, their Lordships made it clear that if Mr. Cube had incurred his expenditure simply to prevent a change in the ownership of the Company's share capital, then this would not have been a justifiable advertising expenditure. While this may lead other companies into future difficulties, the Tate and Lyle case has established at the very minimum that heavy expenditures undertaken by any firm threatened by public ownership have a very good chance of being treated as expenses for tax purposes.

While there is some support in the Labour Party for remedial legislation to deal with party-related propaganda, it would be difficult if not impossible to legislate in prohibition of generalised institutional advertising such as, for example, the Free Enterprise Campaign. Politics is involved on both sides of the issue ; restriction of advertising and public relations activities with political overtones can become invasion of freedom of opinion and expression.

Whatever the future of public relations in Britain at the present time, British industry has a clear advantage in the whole area of propaganda over the Labour Party. There has never been any prohibition, beyond what its articles of association may contain, on what a company may spend on political advertising between elections. The only deterrents have been taxation—never strong and far weaker now that Tate and Lyle's have won their case—and the election law which, as the Tronoh Mines case has demonstrated, does not in fact prohibit expenditures during the few weeks of a general election campaign. While it is too early to anticipate the effects of these decisions on the volume of free enterprise advertising and publicity, once its benefits have been demonstrated there can be no question that industry can place tremendous financial resources behind the effort. And, unlike the Labour Party which is experiencing a period of debate and uncertainty, British industry knows exactly what it wants and can enlist considerable expertise to put its case. Whether or not, in the words of a speaker at the 1951 International Advertising Conference,

> ' the great truths of civilised living and happiness, the major principles of peace and prosperity, the wisdom of the world's wisest men, can be packaged and presented, distributed and sold as cornflakes are sold, by tried and proven commercial methods,'[1]

free enterprise in Britain can be and is ' packaged and presented, distributed and sold . . .'.

It is significant that most of the industries mentioned in the Labour Party's 1953 policy statement ' Challenge to Britain ' have either planned or started public relations campaigns. In November, 1953, the chairman of the Fairey Aviation Company promised share holders that ' any steps that might be taken to protect your interests against that risk (of nationalisation) are under consideration '. I.C.I., the largest British chemical firm, issued a detailed refutation of Labour's case for public ownership which was circulated to shareholders and the press. This was followed up, as Tate and Lyle had done three years before, by the establishment of a profit-sharing scheme for employees. Mr. Rogerson, then chairman of I.C.I., used the occasion of the 1953 Annual General Meeting to renew the assurance given by Lord McGowan in

[1] *Scope*, September, 1951, p. 114.

1949 that ' the Board would take all proper steps to oppose the nationalisation of your Company if the attempt were ever made '.

Finally, the chairman of Alfred Herbert's, one of the largest manufacturers in the machine tool industry, also marked down for public ownership by the Labour Party, outlined a programme of resistance which the Labour Party can scarcely ignore:

> ' First I think that we as individuals and in our political and trade associations must actively engage in a campaign to defeat the menace which hangs over us by making it clear to our voters that nationalisation is a direct threat to progress, prosperity and full employment.
>
> ' Next, if the menace comes nearer every company and every individual concerned must fight relentlessly for freedom. . . . By and large I think we are a fairly tough set of individuals and not likely to sacrifice our liberties and placidly to submit to the dictation of political boards. . . ".[1]

Meanwhile, the Labour Party continues to rely upon the traditional loyalty of the British working class and the support of marginal middle-class groups. To these elements, of course, Socialism has always seemed to offer security and abundance, and the more obvious kinds of Party propaganda have been of less importance. The Labour Government, however, was unable to dispense with rationing and shortages, and under pressure from various economic and Cold War problems, unable to proceed with the full-scale reconstruction of British society. Meanwhile the Conservative Government, operating under far easier conditions, has demonstrated that, at least temporarily, prosperity and solvency can be associated with free markets, decontrol and full employment.

It is against this background that industry public relations must be evaluated. It argues, not so much that it can do the job better (there is large agreement on the nature of the economic problems), but that it can do the job as well. If Socialism offers people ' Fair Shares ' and levelling-upward, free enterprise presents, says the Institute of Directors, consumer choice and ' the chance to get on ', and, it adds, the State is remote and indirect ;

---

[1] *Machine Tool Review.* ' Nationalisation ? ' Alfred S. Herbert, July–August, 1953.

industry is close and personal. Better trust business than bureaucracy. In large measure, therefore, the burden of proof is thrust on the Socialists. ' Why change ' ? is the real message of the thousands of advertisements and newspaper stories. The Labour Party, once again and in somewhat new terms, must state the case.

CHAPTER VIII

IMPACT OF NATIONALISATION

' We are about to take over the mining industry. It is not so easy as it looks. I have been talking about nationalisation for forty years but the implications of the transfer of property have never occurred to me.' EMANUEL SHINWELL, Minister of Fuel and Power, November 22, 1945.

With the exceptions of steel and certain sections of transport, the debate on the Labour Party's nationalisation programme was largely confined to the uses and abuses of party politics. Only two of the nationalisation measures related to productive industries, as distinct from services, and so far as the coal industry was concerned the case for nationalisation or quasi-nationalisation was not seriously questioned.[1] As the *Economist* noted, in August, 1945,

' Support for the principle of public ownership of the mines is now very wide, extending probably to two and a half of the three parties.'[2]

Nationalisation of the Bank of England was supported by several Conservatives,[3] and, presumably, received the tacit approval of the Leader of the Opposition, Mr. Churchill.[4] It was also ' diffi-

[1] Thus even the F.B.I. admitted that the ' coal industry needed special treatment '. Sir Clive Baillieu, President of the F.B.I. ' Industry : Plans and Prospects ', address to a General Meeting of Members of the Midland Region of the Federation, at Birmingham, July 25, 1947, p. 3. Aside from nationalisation of transport and iron and steel, which it opposed, the Federation largely confined itself to criticising details in the nationalisation measures.

[2] *Economist*, August 18, 1945, p. 220.

[3] One Conservative, Robert Boothby, actually voted for the Act nationalising the Bank without, apparently, any repercussions in the Party. I. J. Pitman, Conservative M.P. and a former director of the Bank, described the compensation as ' eminently fair ' (*Hansard*, Vol. 415, Col. 65, October 29, 1945). ' No one,' wrote Quinton Hogg (Lord Hailsham), an influential member of the Party, ' is much better or worse off as the result of what can only be described as an elaborate game of make-believe.' *The Case for Conservatism* (London, 1947), p. 154.

[4] The ' national ownership of the Bank of England ', Churchill was quoted, ' does not, in my opinion, raise any matter of principle. . . . There are important examples in the United States and in our dominions of central banking institutions.' *Hansard*, Vol. 43, Col. 93. August 16, 1945. It is also suggestive that he did not attend the debate on the Second Reading of the Bank Bill, and did not vote on the measure.

cult for anyone to get very excited ' about nationalisation of civil aviation, which had already been partly nationalised, or cable and wireless, which were issues ' at or near the margin of indifference '.[1] Summing up the nationalisation programme, the *Economist* was able to conclude that it represented not too much but almost too little. ' The country,' it commented in November, 1945,

> ' very clearly expressed its preference for a Labour Government over any other possibility, and the voters were not so naive as to imagine that they could get a Labour Government without a Socialist policy. . . . From this point of view Mr. Morrison's list is most moderately short. An avowedly Socialist Government, with a clear Parliamentary majority, might well have been expected to go several steps further. There is nothing in the list about the land . . . ocean-going shipping . . . and many who are not Socialists would welcome a large measure of public ownership, as distinct from operation, of merchant shipping. . . . The socialisation of the fuel and power industries strangely omits any mention of petroleum which, in its domestic aspects, might be thought the most obvious target of all. Nothing is said about any sections of the food distributing industry—such, for example, as milk distribution. Clearly, Mr. Morrison might have gone a great deal further.
>
> ' There is thus no call for anyone who survived without terror the shock of the election results to feel alarm now. If there is to be a Labour Government, the programme now stated is almost the least it could do without violating its election pledges.'[2]

The ease with which the nationalisation programme was accepted is partly explained by the conditions prevailing in the industries, the majority of which had been State-aided, or subject to a measure of control, for a considerable period.[3] It was also true, as Robert Brady has suggested, that

---

[1] *Economist*, November 10, 1945, pp. 668–669.

[2] Ibid., November 24, 1945, p. 739.

[3] Pre-war nationalisation or quasi-nationalisation in Britain has been treated in Ernest Davies, *National Capitalism* (London, 1939), W. A. Robson, ed., *Public Enterprise* (London, 1937).

' all of the nationalisation, or semi-nationalisation programmes were based squarely on findings, and in large part
on recommendations, which had been made by Conservative-
dominated fact-finding and special investigating committees.
This was true of the Bank of England (MacMillan report),
coal (Reid report), gas (Heyworth report), electricity
(McGowan report). . . .'[1]

Finally, the nationalisation measures themselves did not contem-
plate for the most part a transfer of power from existing managerial
elements to new ruling groups.[2] As long as relationships within
the industries were left fundamentally unchanged, it was clear
that nationalisation in certain cases would be acceptable to influential elements in Britain.[3]

On the other hand, it is not quite correct that

' nationalisation of the iron and steel industry seems to have
been mainly the nationalisation of a plan for reorganising
the industry which had been advanced by the Iron and Steel
Federation itself.'[4]

The various nationalisation measures, of course, did not propose
the transfer of authority to workers' representatives under the
general supervision of the Government, and, in fact, the steel
measure effected much less a departure from the *status quo ante*
than had been achieved by other Acts of nationalisation. Never-

---

[1] Robert A. Brady, *Crisis In Britain* (Berkeley, 1950), p. 41.

[2] This aspect of nationalisation has been extensively discussed. See, for example,
Men on the Boards (Acton Society Trust, 1951) ; Hugh Clegg, *Industrial Democracy
and Nationalisation* (Oxford, 1951) ; A. M. de Neuman, *Consumers' Representation in
the Public Sector of Industry* (Cambridge, 1950).

[3] The principal concern was that the area of managerial authority should not be
circumscribed under public or private ownership. Thus, according to S. A. Dismore,
who had been the ' financial brain behind Imperial Airways' affairs ', with regard to
aviation, ' The secret of success . . . remains unchanged by nationalisation. Pick
keen directors and executives, tell them the task (and make it hard enough), give
them the necessary power and above all trust them. . .'. Quoted in John Longhurst,
Nationalisation in Practice : the Civil Aviation Experiment. (London, 1950), p. 89.
Similarly, the *Economist* rejected ' political nationalisation ', represented by the Post
Office, and management by Government, workers' and consumers' representatives
as methods of control in the nationalised industries. ' The best way to run a nationalised coal industry ', it suggested, ' is to seek out a body of men of the highest
personal qualities, to require them to be, or become, entirely independent of all the
interests concerned, and then to leave as much as possible to their unfettered dis-
cretion and judgment.' *Economist*, October 6, 1945, pp. 474–475.

[4] Brady, op. cit., p. 41.

theless, nationalisation of steel went well beyond the plan which the industry had advanced for itself, and occasioned the most bitter controversy of the entire six-year period of office of the Labour Government. The ability of a determined and unwilling industry to resist nationalisation, which the struggle for steel demonstrated, raises questions of profound importance for future policy.

It must be stated, however, as a factor of importance in the dispute, that to the British public the Labour case for steel nationalisation was rather less conclusive than the arguments that had been advanced for nationalisation of other industries.[1] To begin with, from 1939 until 1948 the steel industry had been subject to a measure of public control which, so far as the public was concerned, seemed to have accomplished the objectives of the nationalisation Act, thereby rendering the Act unnecessary. Moreover, unlike the coal, gas, and electricity industries, steel had not been the subject of a number of impartial reports critical of the industry and suggesting major changes in organisation or policy. There was little to criticise in the industry's record during and since the war, and the Labour Government, therefore, was forced to rely for its arguments on pre-war developments within the industry which, by 1948, seemed almost ancient history. Nor was the Labour case helped by frequent ' leaks ' to the press of a division in the Cabinet on the question of nationalisation with, it was alleged, the ' moderate ' wing led by Attlee and Morrison opposing the ' left ' wing pro-nationalisation faction headed by Dalton and Bevan.[2] The Conservative Party, mean-

---

[1] For the general Labour view on steel nationalisation consult G. D. H. Cole, *Why Nationalise Steel?* (New Statesman Pamphlet ; London, 1948) ; Wilfred Fienburgh and Richard Evely, *Steel is Power* : *The Case for Nationalisation* (London, 1948) ; and the various publications of the Labour Party, especially *Britain's Steel at Britain's Service* (n.d.).

[2] Thus it was popular to regard the Steel Bill as ' primarily a sop to Cerberus, a ransom paid to radical insistence. . . Mr. Attlee, Mr. Morrison, and Sir Stafford Cripps at any rate can have no illusions about what they have agreed to do. . . Pressure on the Cabinet this year has no doubt been reinforced by the return of Mr. Dalton and by the shrewd and successful demagogy of Mr. Bevan . . .' *The Times*, September 4, 1948. According to the *Manchester Guardian* of October 30, 1948, ' the steel industry had to be nationalised to satisfy the yearning of the Left Wing. . . .' The *Economist* of November 6, 1948, maintained that the decision was taken ' because a handful of Ministers . . . have established a moral ascendency over the majority of their colleagues. . . . The introduction of the Steel Bill is the clearest example west of the iron curtain of the way in which a minority within a minority can achieve its aims '.

while, declared its intention to de-nationalise the industry at the first opportunity. These and other considerations strengthened the steel industry's opposition to nationalisation, and were, perhaps, responsible for carrying the opposition further than it would otherwise have gone.

The industry's principal defence, however, was with reference to the war and post-war period. Steel nationalisation, it contended, did not take into account that

' By a process of trial and error over the last fifteen years, the Industry and the Government have between them succeeded in working out a sound relationship between Government supervision and private enterprise—one of the cardinal problems of present-day industrial policy. Its soundness has been proved by the high production, high productivity and swift progress with a development plan of unprecedented size which the industry has achieved since the war. This successful experiment in industrial statecraft is being discarded, before its lessons have been fully learned, in favour of an untried system with many obvious defects.'[1]

The present system of control, the industry suggested, exercised full supervision over the price structure and development policy of the industry, and if

' these powers were, in the Government's view, insufficient, they could have been increased without disturbing the effective and fruitful partnership which had been developed.[2]

The chief element in the control which had been established by the Labour Government prior to nationalisation was the Iron and Steel Control Board,[3] organised in September, 1946, to

---

[1] *Iron and Steel Bill : Some Arguments For and Against.* (Iron and Steel Federation).
[2] loc. cit.

[3] The *Financial Times's* ' Observer ', in his column of May 5, 1947, described the Iron and Steel Control Board as ' that body of Trojan donkeys . . . taking credit for the development plans drawn up by the Steel Federation . . . doodling at the taxpayer's expense '. The comment that follows, which was directed at the Board's chairman, is also illustrative of the atmosphere in which Government-appointed steel controllers had to operate. ' How odd it is,' ' Observer ' continued, ' that the Finance Director, and a former managing director, of Spillers should be the instrument for nationalising steel ! If there is any logic in Sir Archibald Forbes's conduct in being chairman of a Board whose purpose is to eliminate private enterprise from (continued on next page)

replace the war-created Iron and Steel Control of the Ministry of Supply. Under the chairmanship of Sir Archibald Forbes, Managing Director of Spillers and, subsequently, President of the F.B.I., the Board consisted of two directors of steel companies, including the President-elect of the Iron and Steel Federation, one shipbuilding, two trade union representatives and two civil servants, all of whom were appointed for a two-year period. Its duties, according to a Government statement, were

> ' To review and supervise programmes of development needed for the modernisation of the iron and steel industry and to watch over the execution of approved schemes in such programmes. To supervise as necessary the industry in current matters, including the provision of its raw material requirements, and the administration, under powers delegated by the Minister, of such continued direct control as may be required over the production, distribution and import of iron and steel products. To advise on general price policy for the industry and on the fixing of prices for controlled products.'[1]

The Board's terms of reference suggested it enjoyed broad authority over the industry, but in fact, as the industry itself admitted, it exercised even fewer powers than the war-time Iron and Steel Control. ' Unlike the Control,' a Steel Federation publication has commented, the Board

> ' did not in general concern itself with the detailed execution of policy, but left this to the Federation and subsidiary organisations of the industry.'[2]

---

steel, surely it follows that Mr. Strachey (Minister of Food) should take over the profitable business of Spillers, which requires much less management than the steel industry. Spillers' shareholders would do well to consider asking Sir Archibald about his intentions. If he is convinced of the virtues of nationalisation, surely he ought to devote all his time and the rest of his life to the task. Or will Sir Archibald return to the managing directorship of Spillers in time for Mr. Strachey to make use of his nationalising talents in the milling industry ? '.

[1] *Board of Trade Journal*, September 14, 1946, p. 1256.

[2] *Iron and Steel Bill : Some Arguments For and Against*, p. 30. This conclusion is at some variance with another comment in the same publication (p. 14) which suggests that ' supervision has actually involved the making by the Board, almost daily, of positive suggestions about the current problems of the industry '. How it could make positive suggestions ' almost daily ', without concerning itself with ' detailed execution of policy ' was not explained.

It was also true—and portentous—that on a number of occasions the Board's efforts to exert its authority were successfully resisted by the Federation, particularly with reference to import policy. Thus there is some ground for believing that the perpetuation of the control would have led, in fact, to

> ' serious clashes on matters of major policy between private and public interests . . . possibly with the gravest consequences.'[1]

The industry's development plan, on the other hand, raised issues of a different sort. Put forward in late 1945 in response to a Caretaker Government request in May of that year, the plan contemplated an expenditure by the industry of £168 million at then current price levels over a period of $7\frac{1}{2}$ years, to reach an output capacity of 16 million tons,

> ' giving a production of 15,000,000 tons after allowing some 6 per cent for the difference which would normally be expected between capacity and realised output.'[2]

As originally conceived, the plan was based on an expected demand for steel by 1953 of 13 million tons for home consumption and 3 million tons for export. At first glance, the plan which involved a production expansion of about one-third in a little over seven years seemed to demonstrate that the industry had, in fact, adjusted to new conditions. Although it was described as a ' Death Bed Repentence ' because it had not been produced earlier, the Labour Party admitted that it was ' a good technical piece of work '.[3]

Examined more closely, however, the industry's development plan was found to rest on a number of doubtful assumptions. Perhaps the most important of these—and one which was quickly disproved—was the estimate of needed capacity by 1953. By 1951 the industry was already producing over 16 million tons annually, and there was a continuing desperate shortage of steel which, even without rearmament, would have been in short

---

[1] Minister of Supply in (Daily) *Hansard*, Vol. 458, No. 15, Col. 57. February 15, 1948.
[2] Iron and Steel Federation, *Report to the Minister of Supply on the Iron and Steel Industry*, December, 1945. p. 14.   [3] *Britain's Steel at Britain's Service*, p. 12.

M

supply. It was evident, in other words, that the development plan had been too narrowly conceived, if only because the production target based on estimated need in 1953 was achieved in 1950 and proved, at that time, incapable of satisfying demand. Afterthought, of course, is more certain than prophecy, but it should be noted that as early as July 1948, G. D. H. Cole amongst others had criticised the plan as grossly insufficient, and concluded that

> ' Persons who could put forward such an estimate are plainly not to be trusted to control the reorganisation of an industry on which, more than on any other save coal, the economic survival of Great Britain depends.'[1]

It was also a questionable assumption, in the context of the nationalisation debate, that the development plan as a ' free enterprise achievement ' should depend on substantial Government financing. Of a contemplated annual expenditure of £22½ million for 7½ years, the industry proposed to provide between £6 million and £7 million annually. £10 million, it was noted, might possibly be available in funds provided by the Government for repairs which had been deferred during the war. Half the cost of the programme, the Steel Federation concluded, could be met out of the industry's own resources. It was clear that the remaining half, or £84 million of the original estimate,[2] would be largely financed by the Government.[3]

A further assumption of the Development Plan was that the Iron and Steel Federation was the proper organ to rationalise the entire industry and assign individual steel producers their respective roles in the plan. There was, however, some resistance to Federation control within the industry. ' We have continuously opposed the Federation's proposals,' one steel company chairman declared,

> ' as affecting our own works . . . we take the view that we

---

[1] Cole, op. cit., p. 20.

[2] The estimate of £168 million was eventually raised to £200 million.

[3] The industry's attempts to raise capital from private sources were not very successful, e.g., over 90 per cent of an issue of 3 per cent 10-year Debentures by the Steel Company of Wales in 1947 was left unsubscribed, provoking a *Daily Express* (July 17, 1947) description as ' the biggest non-gilt-edged new issue flop since the War '.

ourselves know best the particular necessities of our own plant.'[1]

Another company, in a letter read by the Ministry of Supply to the House of Commons, declared that it entirely disagreed

' with the implications . . . in the report as to the future of these works . . . and the Chairman of this Company . . . has already written to the British Iron and Steel Federation . . . to this effect.'[2]

Thus the Government was strengthened in its conviction that while a

' certain amount can be done, and is being done now, by voluntary agreement under the Development Plan. . . . It is at the next and subsequent stages, when the first urgent improvements have been carried out and the further steps for re-organising the industry have to be settled and implemented, that the sectional interests of multiple owners inevitably stand in the way. To nationalise the industry properly, and so get the maximum efficiency, a single owner must replace the many. . . .'[3]

It was, of course, true that by the time the steel nationalisation measure was given its Second Reading in November, 1948, the technical case for and against nationalisation that has been discussed was obscured by larger issues. The almost continual debate that had been carried on since 1945 had served to focus public attention on steel nationalisation more than on any other industrial policy or programme of the Labour Government. For many on both sides of the question steel nationalisation had come to symbolise the basic doctrines and traditions of the respective parties, and for almost the first time since the war, to get at the roots of the difference between the parties. Steel nationalisation was also the occasion of the most determined struggle for power between the Labour Government, on the one

---

[1] Chairman of the South Durham Steel Works to the Annual General Meeting, reported in the *Financial Times*, May 24, 1946, quoted in Fienburgh and Evely, op. cit., p. 92.

[2] Quoted in ibid.

[3] Minister of Supply (Daily) *Hansard*, Vol. 458, No. 15, November 15, 1948, Col. 59.

hand, and British industry on the other, represented by the Iron and Steel Federation. To the Labour Party steel was an important test of whether the present and future programmes of the Party could be successfully carried through against powerful opposition. To industry, steel was the issue upon which the whole future of British free enterprise depended, and the point at which the struggle between fundamentally different philosophies, hitherto muted or confused, was finally joined. It was broadly recognised by all sides that the monopoly, inefficiency, and pre-war history arguments for nationalisation were less important than the fact that ownership and control of the industry gave crucial power over the economy to the Government. In the end, moreover, it was the recognition of this by the Steel Federation and their political and industrial allies that prevented the transformation of the nationalisation Act into effective Government operation of the industry.

When the Steel Bill was debated in late 1948, the Iron and Steel Control Board had already been disbanded, following the refusal of all but the trade union members to accept reappointment for an additional year, ' because of their opposition to Government policy '.[1]

As introduced, the Steel Bill provided for the transfer to a public Iron and Steel Corporation of the securities of 83 parent and 24 subsidiary steel companies producing above a datum level, with regard to most types of production, of 20,000 tons. It was estimated that the Corporation would thereby acquire control of the bulk of the industry including the following proportions of major products :

					%
iron ore	..	..	..	..	97.5
pig iron	..	..	..	..	97.6
ingot steel	..	..	..	..	99.3
hot-rolled products	..	..	..	93.6[2]

[1] Minister of Supply (Daily) *Hansard*, Vol. 458, No. 15, Col. 57, November 15, 1948.

[2] It is interesting, for purposes of comparison, that the total output of the nationalised industry, it was estimated, would be ' half the present output of the United States Steel Corporation, and little more than half that of the Bethlehem Steel Corporation and the Republic Steel Corporation '. Minister of Supply (Daily) *Hansard*, Vol. 458, No. 15, Col. 77, November 15, 1948.

Compensation for the companies acquired was based on stock market valuations of the shares on alternate dates in 1945 and 1948, and would provide, according to the Minister of Supply, that

> ' nearly all shareholders who have bought their shares within the last 10 years or so will receive in compensation more than they paid for them.'[1]

The debate on the measure occupied 36 meetings in Committee and 4 sittings at the Report stage. Opposition motions were defeated by comfortable majorities, and the Bill was given a Third and Final Reading in May, 1949. It had been expected that the Bill would not receive approval from the House of Lords,[2] and although the Government rejected a number of Lords amendments, the Lords continued to insist that the amendments be accepted. Finally, a compromise was worked out which provided that in return for the House of Lords' approval of the Bill, no person would be appointed to the Corporation before 1 October, 1950, and no properties would be transferred to the Corporation before January 1, 1951. Eventually, the Government chose February 15, 1951, as the date on which the industry would be vested in the Corporation.

The compromise, of course, was designed to postpone nationalisation until after the General Election which, in accordance with British electoral law, was scheduled in early 1950. The February, 1950, General Election, however, returned the Labour Government, although with its majority reduced to 6 seats in the House of Commons, and on 15 February, 1951, after months of fierce Parliamentary opposition, the iron and steel industry was formally reconstituted as the Iron and Steel Corporation.

Under the terms of the Act,[3] the Corporation was to consist

---

[1] ibid., Col. 70.

[2] Under the Parliament Act of 1911, the House of Lords retained the power to delay for two years the passage of any legislation, other than a Finance Bill. In November 1947, the Labour Government introduced a new Parliament Bill to cut the Lords' delaying power to one year. Since the Bill was opposed in the Lords, it was itself subject to the two year delay period provided for by the 1911 Act and did not receive the Royal Assent until December 1949. It is obvious from the timing of this measure that it came too late to influence the passage of the Iron and Steel Bill.

[3] Iron and Steel Act (1949), 12 and 13 Geo. 6 Ch. 72.

of a chairman and between six and ten other members chosen by the Minister of Supply

> ' from amongst persons appearing to him to be persons who have had a wide experience of, and shown capacity in, the production of iron ore or iron and steel, industrial, commercial or financial matters, administration or the organisation of workers.'[1]

Extended powers were given to the Corporation to discontinue or restrict the activities, or to dispose of all or any of the assets, of the publicly-owned companies; to carry out reorganisation and development for the industry as a whole ; to promote research, and the education and training of persons employed by the Corporation or the separate companies.

With regard to internal organisation, the Iron and Steel Act was designed to effect as large a measure of autonomy for the industry as was consistent with overall direction. Although the Corporation enjoyed the power to remove and appoint directors, it had been insisted during the debate that in general the directors affected would be those who held non-executive directorships and/or multiple directorships. The Steel Bill, the *Manchester Guardian* had noted,

> ' gives the impression that little will change in the steelworks. Companies remain intact, boards of directors stay in office and continue to be whipped along by the profit motive, except that they will be responsible to the State and not to private shareholders.'[2]

Whether or not, therefore, nationalisation was not necessary except to ' keep the Labour Party together ', it was not intended to effect major changes in the industry : the principal change was the transfer of steel securities from private to public ownership. The actual transfer in February, 1951, was hardly noticed by the general public. During succeeding months, so far as the public was aware, nationalisation of the industry was evident only in the resignation from some companies of a small number of directors in accordance with Corporation policy.

[1] Part I, Section 1 (2).
[2] *Manchester Guardian*, October 30, 1948.

In fact, however, both before and after nationalisation of the industry, the Government and the Federation were engaged in a determined struggle for power in the industry. Notwithstanding the numerous concessions made to the Conservative Opposition and industry organisations during the debate, the Iron and Steel Federation steadily refused co-operation. Only one member of the Corporation was appointed from the industry, and he had formerly been attached to one of the smaller companies. Nor was this the decision of the Government. ' I was anxious,' the Minister of Supply stated in September, 1950,

' as were the Government, to have some leaders of the industry serving on the Corporation. I therefore invited their spokesmen to submit to me the names of experienced men who would be acceptable to their fellow industrialists for inclusion. However, the Executive Committee (of the Steel Federation) decided that such a list would not be submitted to me . . . and they warned me at the same time that the Corporation, deprived of such people, would be unable successfully to plan the steel industry. Furthermore, I was informed that every effort would be made to dissuade any important man I might approach from serving on the Corporation. . . . This is concerted action by a number of people for sabotaging an Act of Parliament.'[1]

As chairman of the Iron and Steel Control Board, and, later, chairman of the industry, the Government had originally solicited the services of Dr. Van der Bijl, Chairman of the South African Iron and Steel Industrial Corporation. Dr. Van der Bijl had been sufficiently interested to spend some months in Britain in 1946, but after talks had declined appointment on account of ' pressing interests in South Africa '. Subsequently, the Government had talked directly to steel company managers but without success. In the end, Steven J. L. Hardie, Chairman of the British Oxygen Company, Ltd., who had joined the Labour Party in 1946, was appointed to head the Corporation.[2] At no time did the

---

[1] Quoted in the *New Statesman and Nation*, September 23, 1950, p. 285.

[2] Hardie, who raised British Oxygen to a monopoly position in the industry, and who had a reputation for unusual strength of character, was thought to have had a proper background for dealing with the Iron and Steel Federation.

Federation suggest a nominee for the position, although at one time, it was rumoured, the Federation's chairman, Sir Andrew Duncan, had been considered for the post.

Similarly, during an interim period after the vesting date, the Steel Federation refused to permit representatives of the Corporation to sit on Federation Committees and participate in their activities.[1] Corporation representatives were also prohibited from membership on the Federation's Council, and until July, 1951 the Federation would not permit the Corporation to acquire control or be represented on the boards of subsidiary companies of the Federation through which it purchased on behalf of the entire industry iron ore, scrap, and other steel-making materials. In July, 1951, by an agreement that was described as an ' armed truce ',[2] the Federation agreed to permit Corporation representation on the boards of the subsidiary companies.

It may be suggested, therefore, that the comment in the industry publication *Iron and Steel* in March, 1951, was an understatement. ' In effect,' the journal noted, a month after nationalisation,

> ' the Federation will continue to discharge the functions it has had under private enterprise while the Corporation remains *in statu pupillari*.'[3]

The existing controllers, it added, will continue to run the industry

> ' while members of the newly constituted Steel Corporation are learning the difference between steel and slag. . . .'[4]

The remarkable fact, however, is not that the opposition of the industry continued after nationalisation, or even that the industry undertook to thwart nationalisation systematically, but that the Government was silent and powerless in the face of the challenge. It must be stated, of course, that the political atmo-

---

[1] In February, 1951, the Minister of Supply had indicated that there would be an interim period of three months following the vesting date during which Corporation representatives would sit on the Federation's Committees. A short time later the Corporation announced that it had been unable to reach agreement with the Federation on the matter. *The Times*, February 17, 1951.

[2] *Manchester Guardian*, July 14, 1951.

[3] *Iron and Steel*. Vol. 24, No. 3 (March, 1951), p. 73.

[4] ibid., p. 104.

sphere was not conducive to a ' showdown '. It was confidently expected after February, 1950, that the new Labour Government would not long remain in office, and that one of the first actions of a Conservative Government would be the denationalisation of steel. A number of companies such as Vickers and Cammell Laird, whose steel business had been nationalised, revealed that the compensation received had been placed in separate funds which would be used for the repurchase of steel affiliates in the event of a Conservative victory.[1] There was also a possibility that any Government effort effectively to nationalise the industry would precipitate the mass resignation of industry executives and managers, which the Government, resting on a slim Parliamentary majority, was not prepared to risk.

It is also important that throughout the entire period the press neglected to present the issues that were posed. Except in Socialist organs the Government's case for nationalisation was never fully treated, and after formal nationalisation of the industry the running dispute between the Corporation and the Federation reflected, so far as the press was concerned, only discredit on the Government. The *Economist*, for example, was led to observe in June, 1951, that

' the Federation has won the first sparring rounds ; and it may be that its leaders would like to tempt Mr. Hardie into really intemperate action. They may even succeed in this. But the consequences would be a damaging illustration of the folly of the Government in making the steel industry the plaything of politics.'[2]

Successive statements of the Minister of Supply, which have been referred to, were not fully reported, while at the same time statements by Federation officials were usually published in their entirety. As a result, the public to a large extent remained unaware that the Federation was engaged in what may be termed active non-co-operation, or that there were outstanding differences between the Government and the Federation. Thus the Government could not be certain of support in any crisis that developed

---

[1] In 1954 Vickers and Cammell Laird bought back the ordinary share capital of the English Steel Co., which they had previously owned.

[2] *Economist*, June 30, 1951.

in the industry. Cast in the role of intruder and interloper, it was severely handicapped from the outset in its struggle with the Federation.

Nevertheless, two major criticisms can be made of the Government's handling of the whole problem of steel nationalisation. In the first place, as the *New Statesman and Nation* noted in June, 1951, it was

> ' paying the price for deferring the one really controversial item in its nationalisation programme to the dying days of the last Parliament. . . .'[1]

By 1948 the popular enthusiasm and support which had attended the 1945 General Election had largely evaporated, and certainly by 1950 nationalisation in principle was an evocative slogan only in some circles in the Labour Party. Building and re-equipment in the industries taken over had precluded, in most cases, price reductions and some other benefits which, the public had been led to believe, would inevitably result from nationalisation. At the same time, the workers in the industries had not been accorded a new status or responsibility. There was, therefore, no reserve of popular acclaim when steel nationalisation was undertaken.

It may be suggested also that the Government did not pursue the advantages it possessed in the struggle with the Federation. The Federation was, and is, supported by levies on the industry, and the bulk of its finances after nationalisation were contributed by the publicly-owned companies. It was also true that its governing bodies were composed in the main of representatives of the nationalised companies. Yet, as far as could be learned, the Government did not use these powers to influence, let alone control, Federation policy. There was, at least, no sign of such influence or control, and meanwhile the publicly-owned companies continued to finance the Federation and be represented in it.

With the advent of a Conservative Government in October, 1951, the reorganisation of the industry on the basis of public ownership was abruptly halted and by the end of 1954, the Churchill Government had successfully denationalised about one half of the steel industry. The Labour Party, if returned to power, is

[1] *New Statesman and Nation*, June 30, 1951, p. 737.

committed to nationalise the industry once again. Much depends, of course, on whether Labour can ever recapture the popular mood that produced its 1945 victory. If and when that time comes, it is possible that the steel industry, and industry generally, will bow to the inevitable in accordance with the traditions of social change in Britain.

But it is far from certain that the transition from the Welfare State to the Socialist Commonwealth can be accomplished without violence being done to the traditions and customs of British democracy. The steel dispute, at least, suggests that some of the effective limits of planning are determined not at the ballot box or by the planners themselves, but by the power interests of affected groups. To the extent, however, that any further development of British Socialism is aimed at the socialisation of power, it will have to overcome, by one means or another, an industrial opposition utilising every obstructionist technique at its command. At the same time, it may also be necessary to replace existing managerial cadres hostile to State control with skilled personnel whose co-operation is assured. Timing, of course, is of the essence ; and much, too, depends on the character and wisdom of a newer political and industrial leadership.

In the end, however, the socialisation of power may require a conscious choice between a stalemate which leaves intact the status quo, and an advance bought at the risk of upsetting both the political and economic stability of British society. Faced with this choice in the case of steel, the Labour Government hesitated and temporised at the expense of effective nationalisation of the industry, and thereby suffered defeat. It is at least debatable, assuming that the power issue will re-emerge at every important stage of the progress from a planned economy to socialism, whether at the first real test the Labour Government should not have taken a clear and forthright decision. An attempt to avoid this issue, R. H. Tawney suggested in 1945, would have dire consequences, not merely for the Labour experiment but for the world struggle between competing solutions to economic and social problems. For the ' economic system ', he reminded a Fabian audience,

' is not a collection of independent undertakings, bargaining on equal terms with each other. It is primarily a power system. It is a hierarchy of authority ; and those who can manipulate the more important levers are directly or indirectly, consciously or unconsciously, the real rulers of their fellows.'[1]

[1] R. H. Tawney, ' We Mean Freedom ', *What Labour Could Do* (Fabian Society Lectures, London, 1945), p. 91.

CHAPTER IX

THE POLITICS OF STALEMATE ?

' It's a very fine country on the whole—finer perhaps than what we give it credit for on the other side. There are several improvements I should like to see introduced ; but the necessity of them doesn't seem to be generally felt as yet. When the necessity of a thing is generally felt they usually manage to accomplish it ; but they seem to feel pretty comfortable about waiting till then.'

HENRY JAMES, *The Portrait of a Lady* (1881).

One one occasion in late 1951 the writer asked a high-ranking civil servant to sum up, if he could, the achievement of the Labour Government. Was it in its essentials, the writer wanted to know, the creation of a mixed economy, Welfare State, Socialism, or something else ? 'Well,' the civil servant began, after a pause, ' I don't really know what to say. I think it will be at least ten years before the Attlee Government can be placed in a true perspective. But at the present time it puts me in mind of nothing so much as the voyage of Columbus in 1492. You will recall that when Columbus set out he didn't know where he was going ; when he arrived he didn't know where he was ; and when he returned he didn't know where he had been. Perhaps,' the civil servant concluded, with a wry smile, ' that answers your question.'

To a certain extent it did, but unfortunately it will not suffice as a conclusion to the present study, although it may serve as a qualification of any summary evaluation. Ten years, indeed, may be too short a time to gain a true perspective of the Labour Government, to know, for example, whether the 1945–51 achievement marked the end of an era of liberal reform or the beginning of an era of democratic Socialism. Nevertheless, any attempt to describe in detail certain features of British planning must be followed by an effort, however tentative and incomplete, to plot, in the image of the civil servant, Columbus' course of discovery.

The image, in fact, is an exact one not merely as used, but in the sense that to many in 1945 the British were embarked on a voyage no less important than that which led Columbus to the new world. The Labour Government, it was thought, would demonstrate the extent to which a democratic society could solve crucial economic and social problems without recourse to the extremism of Right of Left. Whether or not the British ' way ' was exportable, developments in Britain were seen to have ramifications elsewhere, particularly in the world-wide struggle between Communism and the West. The West, or rather Western solutions, it was argued, were on trial in Britain ; and the future of parts of Europe, Asia and Africa might well depend on the outcome.

In particular the British experiment could help to test the validity of two major criticisms that have originated with Left and Right opponents of democratic Socialism. The first of these involved the crucial issue of how far and on what terms ruling groups would support and co-operate with social change which was intended to reduce their power and prestige. In Marxist theory, of course, radical reform which attempts to transform existing class relationships is always followed by counter-revolution. The corollary assumption of a class struggle marked by violence presumes that social progress must be accompanied by an effective, and if necessary ruthless, consolidation of power by the new ruling class. Democratic socialists, on the other hand, and particularly British socialists, have tended to stress that violent revolution is not inevitably a prescription for social change, and that in any case the traditions of British democracy have never made it necessary, and do not to-day make it vital, to choose between one type of dictatorship and another.

Not all British socialists, however, were of this opinion before 1945. Indeed, the role of the Bank of England in the overthrow of the second Labour Government in 1931, and even more, the assaults of Fascism on European democracy in the following decade, suggested to many that any future transfer of power would encounter forceful resistance. As Harold Laski put it in 1935,

' a change in the system of property relations . . . on the historical evidence we have, cannot be accomplished without a revolution.

The transition from feudal to bourgeois society was only accompanied by heavy fighting. There is no reason to suppose, unless we assume that men are now more rational than at any time in the past, that we can transform the foundations of bourgeois society without heavy fighting also ; and the assumption of greater rationality is an illusion born of special historical circumstances and now fading before our eyes.'[1]

A loss of faith in the possibilities of democratic change was also partly responsible for Shaw's early admiration of Mussolini and the Webbs' partial conversion to Stalinism in the middle thirties. The overwhelming majority of British Socialists, however, fully embraced the assumption that Labour Party objectives could be achieved through peaceful and gradualist means, and that the co-operation of the ruling class in the transformation to Socialism was assured.

There was equal conviction that comprehensive planning was fully compatible with democracy. Against the argument that is associated with such prominent anti-planners as von Mises and Hayek that planning if it is to be successful must be carried so far as to restrict not only economic but civil liberties, British Socialists have always assumed that there was no inherent contradiction between planning and freedom. Indeed, at the turn of 1945 the Labour argument took the form of insisting that planning would broaden the area of freedom through the provision of full employment and social security. As the Cold War grew more intense, it was further argued that undemocratic ideologies throve on mass insecurity and discontent. From this point of view planning was not only at one with democracy but a necessary condition for the survival of democracy in the face of the Communist challenge. Thus the critique of the anti-planners was thought by Labour· Party supporters to be without substance in Britain and positively wrong in the context of the world political struggle.

The six-year experience of the Labour Government, however,

---

[1] Harold J. Laski, *The State in Theory and Practice* (New York, 1945), p. 243. In later works, Laski grew optimistic about the possibilities of peaceful social change. The ' revolution by consent ' which he urged throughout the war appeared to him to have been substantially achieved, in the United Kingdom at least, in the Labour Government's victory of 1945.

suggests that the working hypotheses of 1945 are in need of some revision, and cannot be applied to the future with the same confidence as they were used in the past. In the first place, the continued co-operation of vested power groups in measures of social change designed to reduce their power and influence can no longer be taken for granted.

Of course, much of the period 1945–51 was characterised by co-operation, and with the possible exception of steel nationalisation there was no important instance of direct obstruction amounting to sabotage by industry. Nevertheless, business support of the Labour Government was subject to a number of qualifications and conditions, which collectively constitute a price for co-operation which future Labour Governments may not be willing to pay. Industry, for its part, draws a firm line between the Welfare State and Socialism in so far as its own role is concerned. It can be assumed, therefore, that any attempt to push beyond the carefully marked frontiers of the present Welfare State will be met with bitter and sustained opposition by industry.

Until 1948–49, as has been noted, there was little attempt by industry to organise an effective opposition to the Labour Government. To begin with, it was felt that public opinion was still solidly behind the Government, and that any excursion by industry into politics would be badly received. It was also true that the essence of the Government's programme thus far had been reform without essential change. There was, to be sure, incessant grumbling about taxes, controls, bureaucracy and other subjects that have always constituted the businessman's fundamental critique of Government, but below the level of self-conscious pronouncement was a clear understanding that most of the reforms instituted by Labour had been due and overdue. Full employment, whatever its social significance, had meant higher profits and dividends for the owners of industry. There had been no diminution in the status of managers, and indeed, business personnel were being used in large numbers to staff the controls. The larger enterprises, particularly, were benefiting from the general orientation of economic policy which tended to reserve for them the lion's share of licenses, permits, and allocations of raw materials. In short, the Welfare State that had been created by

Labour did not appear to threaten the interests of business, and especially the power interests of big business.

Beginning in 1948–49, however, there was a gradual change in outlook. Underlying subsequent developments was a marked shift in public sentiment away from Labour which generated hopes of a Conservative victory in the next General Election. It also became clear that a further five years for Labour would see an extension of nationalisation, redistribution of income, and controls. Yet there was still some hesitation, and it is in this context that Lord Lyle's campaign against sugar nationalisation was of considerable significance. The organisation of a nation-wide protest against nationalisation was unprecedented and, it should be noted, originally greeted with fear and trembling in some industry circles. But the sky, the tax commissioners, and the public prosecutor did not fall on Lord Lyle, and, moreover, even before the General Election of 1950, it was clear that his anti-nationalisation campaign had achieved some success. Encouraged by his performance, and pushed on by shareholders who had been impressed by the Lyle campaign, the directors of British industry by 1950 had become an active and determined opposition to the Labour Government.

A more insidious attempt by business to divide the industrial from the political wing of the Labour Movement took the form of emphasising the essentially common ground beneath industry and labour, the similarity of interests and objectives, and the necessity of a united front against politicians and bureaucrats, agitators and intellectuals, regardless of Party affiliation. ' What is needed to-day,' one industrialist suggested, in a rather candid statement of the *Realpolitik* underlying this approach,

> ' is not politics, but industrial leadership. Trade Associations, of the right type, with the right leaders, can get together with the leaders of organised labour, and save us from the chaos into which we seem to be drifting.'[1]

Similarly, the efforts of the principal management organisations were directed towards breaking down the allegedly artificial social and economic distinctions between management and labour,

---

[1] C. G. Heywood, President of the Society of British Paint Manufacturers, in *The Spectrum* (1949), p. 46.

N

and the inculcation of mutual understanding and respect. It is not suggested that this approach is bad in itself, only that in the present political context it carries with it implications of some importance for the future of the Labour Party and British Socialism. It is worth repeating a point made earlier, namely, that underlying the recognition of the so-called ' human factor ' in industry is an awareness that any improvement in industrial relations reduces, over the long run, support for radical political solutions. Thus profit-sharing, co-partnership, superannuation and other ameliorative schemes which comprise the new industrial sociology are partly designed to camouflage the nature and sources of power in an industrial society, and thereby to strengthen the position of the managerial and property-owning groups. Indeed, it is hardly an exaggeration to suggest that the effect, if not the entire purpose, of what has been termed ' industrial democracy ' under private auspices has been to by-pass the question of political solutions to social and economic problems.

It would be incorrect, of course, to suggest that the whole of British industry is as yet willing to substitute, say, Elton Mayo for Alfred Marshall. In the main, the philosophy of industry is still closer to the older tradition than it is to conscious managerialism. But it is important to distinguish central from marginal tendencies in order to expose the main trends. The outlooks and attitudes of the older industrial leadership appear to be giving way, particularly in the larger firms, to a sophisticated acceptance of State intervention, trade unions, and welfare measures. A frontal attack on Socialism, it is increasingly recognised, and for that matter, an attempt to steer the Conservative Party back to *laisser-faire*, is less important than the development of techniques to keep control in the changed environment of a Welfare State. From this point of view it is incumbent to form a common managerial front with the bureaucracies of Government and trade unionism, and it has already been noted that through the extension of tripartite consultation and the exchange of personnel between Government and business, this approach between 1945 and 1951 was largely successful.

It was also significant that the non-co-operation of industry with Labour Government policies was largely confined to areas in which questions of control formed the substance of controversy. Of the three major disputes between Government and industry, comprising Development Councils, the nationalisation of steel, and the proposal to restrict dividends, the first two, it is worth noting, involved essentially control rather than property-rights issues. The Development Councils were thought to undermine the position of trade associations, and were rejected mainly for that reason. Steel nationalisation, of course, transferred to the Government a vital control over the economy that had formerly, and notwithstanding forms of regulation, been exercised by the Iron and Steel Federation. The proposal to restrict dividends never reached the legislative stage, but it may be remarked that here, too, the basic critique advanced by industry was that voluntary dividend restraint had worked well ; and it was often put forward, with considerable validity, that in this respect boards of directors had co-operated with the Government at the expense of, and in the face of bitter opposition from, shareholders. Indeed, a remarkable feature of the entire period was that the most notable concessions made by industry to Government or organised labour were invariably those which disadvantaged shareholders, the recognition of which was responsible in 1951 for the formation of a Shareholders' Association as much at odds with management as with the Labour Government.

So far as the future is concerned, this analysis suggests that the issue of co-operation or conflict will be joined at every point at which power interests, rather than property interests, are sharply opposed. There are good reasons to assume, at least, that more can be done, although with growing difficulty, in the direction of income distribution and general egalitarian policy. It is likely, however, that any Labour attempt to effectively socialise control of industry will meet with a resistance hardly less determined or complete than that occasioned by steel nationalisation. Then, of course, the Labour Government went down to defeat, and it is possible that any other challenge from industry in the future will be similarly successful.

There is little in the Labour Government's experience to suggest that displaced power groups or other threatened interests were prepared to carry opposition to the point of attempting to subvert the democratic process. Admittedly there was some talk of violent resistance,[1] but such sentiments were in no sense typical of British business opinion. It was also true that there was the continued and partly illicit export of wealth as individuals and institutions sought to escape the consequences of egalitarian measures. These movements, as already noted, were important in the past and could in the future threaten the stability of a Labour Government. But these attempts at flight, it should be noted, were essentially spontaneous and unorganised, reflecting the lack of confidence of the business community rather than a deliberate attempt to bring about the fall of the Labour Government.

Perhaps the main lesson to be learned from the behaviour of business under the Labour Government is that, faced with disagreeable social change, power interests in a well-established democracy will increasingly enter the arena of politics. If it is organised public opinion which in the last resort is the enemy of private power, then business must increasingly influence opinion into friendly rather than hostile attitudes. If the edge of discontent can be blunted by ' reforms ' carried out by business itself, then business will seek to put its own house in order. If Government agencies seek to enter the policy-making areas previously reserved to industry, then business must learn to manœuvre and to shape its tactics—which may range between the poles of co-operation and boycott—in order to keep control. The choice of tactics and the behaviour that follows will depend closely on political power factors, about which industry will more and more seek to be informed. Thus the degree of unity within the Labour Party, the size of its Parliamentary majority, the length

[1] e.g., Mr. J. Gibson Jarvie, Chairman of the United Dominions Trust, Ltd., ' Should we, by some heaven-sent deliverance, escape war, then we shall have to face our own domestic revolution. It may be bloodless, or it may not, but it must come, and for a variety of reasons, but primarily because the liberty-loving British people won't be content to remain for ever under a dictatorship, even if it were efficient, which our present dictatorship is not.

' I believe the time will come, if the Socialists continue in power and pursue their present lines, when the country will rise up against them.

' I believe in constitutional methods, but I also believe—and I make this statement quite deliberately—that when the government of a country is in the hands of reckless and incompetent megalomaniacs there may come a time when the only possible course is to rebel if the country is to be saved.' Quoted in *New York Times,* October 15th, 1948.

of time it has been in office, and the chances of its defeat at the next Election, will be factors of decisive importance in Government-industry relationships. It can be anticipated then that a serious, hard-fought, but mainly constitutional, struggle between the Labour Party and British industry will continue for many years ahead. The skill that industry has already shown in meeting the challenge of Labour, and the Labour Party's loss of political momentum, further suggest that, failing the evolution of new techniques of control, progress towards the ' Socialist Commonwealth ' can scarcely be achieved as quickly in the future as in the immediate past.

While the Labour Government's experience suggests some modification of the view of Left critics as to the form which power struggles assume in democratic societies, and equally a revision of the assumption of unlimited business co-operation which has hitherto dominated Labour thought, six years of office has left unproved the assumption of Right critics that planning and democracy are fundamentally antagonistic. It has long been debated, an observer of the Labour Government has commented,

> ' whether positive planning and control of economic activity in any considerable detail is compatible with the preservation of healthy, peacetime political democracy. It begins to appear that the test which many have thought was imminent in Great Britain is not, after all, to be made in the near future. The planning which the British are testing is certainly no threat to democracy ; how much it contributes, or is capable of contributing, to the positive direction of the economy is still an open question '[1]

The mixed economy that developed under Labour may be summarised as an attempt to impose certain kinds of planning on a free market economy in order to achieve a balanced distribution of resources, full employment, and a more egalitarian distribution of income.

In the first place, it is to be noted that the Labour Government made limited use of central planning. Planning decisions were

---

[1] Ben W. Lewis, *British Planning and Nationalisation* (New York, 1952), p. 41.

dispersed over literally hundreds of organisations, and apparently were not always subject to unified policy directives. Indeed, Government departments often seemed to pursue contradictory objectives.[1] Planning concepts, of course, have always been compatible with administrative decentralisation, and recent development of planning theory has, in fact, stressed the necessity of avoiding excessive concentration of power at the centre of administration. Central planning, however, has always connoted the central formulation of policy in areas regarded as essential. The Labour Government, as has been shown, delegated key planning decisions to a variety of Government and non-Government organisations, and in other areas refrained from making planning decisions at all.

It is also true that much of Labour Government planning was negative rather than positive, in the sense that controls over the economy were designed, in the main, to prohibit or restrain certain kinds of activity. While industry was encouraged to undertake particular activities, such as savings and exports, in no case could the Government require or force industry to adopt policies deemed essential. Thus, there was no means of enforcing industrial expansion or of securing internal economies within industry, or of distributing earnings between wages and salaries, dividends, and retained profits. To be sure, twilight areas must be distinguished, where controls combined negative and positive aspects. Allocations of raw materials, to take one case, were partly based on agreements to export certain percentages of the finished products. But, it will be recalled, such pressures depended in the main on shortages and ceased to apply as materials became more plentiful.

Finally, it is important to observe that the immediate objectives of Labour Government planning did not envisage a radical re-shaping of British society such as would test the compatibility

---

[1] For example, in January 1951, Sir Hartley Shawcross, President of the Board of Trade, urged a ' dramatic increase ' in textile exports one week after George Strauss, Minister of Supply, warned the industry that it would have to sacrifice labour in the interests of the rearmament programme. Balogh lists other cases, notably the reopening of war-time concentrated gasoline stations on almost the same day that gasoline allocations to private motorists were suspended altogether because of the convertibility crisis. T. Balogh, *Dollar Crisis : Causes and Cure* (Oxford, 1949,) p. 246.

of planning and democracy. Most of the planning, J. A. Schumpeter commented in 1950, ' that has been actually done or suggested has nothing specifically socialist about it unless we adopt a definition of socialism that is much too wide to be of any analytic use '.[1]

It is clear that the Welfare State which developed between 1945 and 1951 was fully compatible with the traditions and customs of Western democracy, and by effecting a reconciliation between equality and liberty, even represents a further and logical development of the democratic creed.

What is not so clear, however, is the capacity of the mixed economy to meet future national needs. Thus far neither the Labour nor the Conservative Governments have evolved policies which offer reasonable assurances that the gap between imports and exports will stay closed. There remains too the question of whether the Sterling Area and in particular the Dominions will in the future continue to accept the economic leadership of the United Kingdom, and there is the further question of how much longer the colonies will be content to contribute dollars in return for Sterling balances in London. There is also the serious problem of growing competition in export markets, as both old and new competitors struggle to enter markets which were once the safe and exclusive preserve of British traders.

Finally there is the continued burden of rearmament, the weight of which is determined as much by the logic of techno-logical developments as by the dangers of the international situation. Whatever the solution to these and other problems may be, it is fairly certain that there can be none which does not require an expansion of Government control in the formerly free area of wages, profits and export policy, and a further extension of the public sector as well. But the pace and extent of such an advance are unusually difficult to assess since the course of the British economy depends more than that of any other nation on events in the outside world.

While external events may thus force a departure from the

---

[1] J. A. Schumpeter, *Capitalism, Socialism, and Democracy* (New York, 3rd edn., 1950), p. 410. In the second edition (1947), he observed of Labour Government planning that ' once more it is a case of administering capitalism . . . ' p. 378.

status quo, in the absence of such pressures the internal strength and stability of the mixed economy and the Welfare State should not be overlooked. After three years of Conservative Government it is apparent that the status quo is as broadly acceptable to the Conservative as it is to the Labour Party. Apart from the denationalisation of road haulage and steel and the gradual removal of controls, the Churchill Government has been content to administer the industrial system bequeathed by Labour.

The Welfare State, it has been noted, does not conflict sharply with the interests of power groups in private industry, and for that reason alone has gained wide acceptance in Conservative political circles. For Conservative political strategists, however, the Welfare State has the positive attraction of a society in which a large measure of class rule and general contentment can co-exist. So far as the future of Socialism is concerned, it is paradoxical that the main obstacle to the creation of a Socialist Commonwealth is now the Welfare State itself and the partially planned economy which developed under the Labour Government.

The point, perhaps, is familiar, and need not be laboured. Certainly it can hardly be disputed that radical movements do not flourish on full stomachs, that in proportion to change and reform, demand for further change and reform decreases, and that those measures of amelioration which Joseph Chamberlain aptly titled ' ransom legislation ' have rarely failed to appease the social instinct that seeks fuller democratic expression. The recognition that reform undercuts revolution has, in fact, constituted the articulate major premise of Conservative supporters of industrial democracy and the Welfare State, and already has had far-reaching effects on the fates of radical movements in Canada, New Zealand, Australia and even the United States. ' Socialist movements,' a study of the Canadian Co-operative Commonwealth Federation truly observes,

> ' are faced with the dilemma of maintaining their stability and social gains, and at the same time sustaining the base for a continual effort to reach their objectives.'[1]

[1] S. M. Lipset, *Agrarian Socialism* : *The Co-operative Commonwealth Federation in Saskatchewan* (Berkeley, 1950), p. 277.

This was also the dilemma of the Labour Party well before its defeat in 1951, and it may be suggested that it is one that will always tend to arise where reforms are effected without any accompanying shift in the morals and values of society. In the absence of any Socialist ethic evocative of mass support, the Labour Government was bound to operate the capitalist or middle-class hierarchy of values that is a characteristic of the acquisitive society. Full employment, for example was regarded less as an end in itself than as an initial instalment of individual material advancement. Similarly, expanded opportunity tended to be interpreted as opportunity to emulate the standards and privileges associated with the middle and upper classes. Access to education, the opportunity to acquire decent housing, the right to improve one's economic and social status, the enjoyment of leisure—these attributes of a middle-class social ethic were in fact given fresh meaning and importance by the Labour Government. The improvement in conditions, however, did not carry with it a transformation of ethics generated at lower social levels and borne upward through the whole society. Instead, there was a permeation downward of the middle-class value system, as, earlier in British history, certain standards of the aristocracy had been absorbed by the rising business class.

Such permeation, in turn, complicates the task of British socialists. It was not entirely foreseen, perhaps, that when granted, aspirations for material security can become retained and stubbornly defended property rights which new possessors protect from new challengers. Partly this explains the indifference, and in some cases the hostility, displayed by the better organised unions of skilled workers to less well organised manual and unskilled workers ; and it also illuminates the lack of interest in problems of colonial peoples shown by the British generally. It also partly underlies the steadily increasing conservatism of the Labour Government between 1945 and 1951. Much of its propaganda during the period, to work harder, to produce more, to save and conserve, and finally to vote Labour, was couched primarily in terms of self-interest.

More important still as an obstacle to future socialist advance is the fact that the major power interests in British society are broadly content with the status quo. To begin with, both the major parties have contributed to present developments, and for reasons of politics and expediency, are committed to their preservation. The trade unions, quite obviously, have a vital interest in the Welfare State. So far as industry is concerned, the belief in *laisser-faire* is largely confined to business members of the Liberal Party. British industry as a whole lacks the sense of adventure and the keen desire for competition which is supposed to characterise American business. It is primarily interested in security and stability, and it has been shown in some detail that the Welfare State in its role of protector and controller contributed in large measure to these objectives. Industry, too, is not willing to give up the quite sizeable benefits that were built into the British economy by the Labour Government.

So viewed, the Welfare State represents an adjustment of conflicting social and economic interests which is acceptable to the major elements that comprise British society. The compromise, of course, does not entirely please industry or labour. The former would prefer that the Welfare State be administered by a Conservative Government, and that there be lower taxes, less bureaucracy, and a shift of bargaining power *vis-à-vis* the trade unions to employers. Labour, it is only fair to comment, places the main emphasis on further improvements in wages, hours, working conditions, and social security. But although neither industry nor labour is prepared to relinquish their respective power positions, the resulting balance is tolerable to both.

The status quo is also reinforced by what may be termed the considerable gap between socialist politics and Socialist thought. It has been commented that proponents of steel nationalisation were forced to rely on arguments that could be proved only by reference to the pre-war history of the industry. Similarly, the rationale of the Labour Government's anti-monopoly policy was essentially that which supported Progressive politics fifty years ago in the United States. Indeed, the whole achievement of the Labour Government was flavoured by assumptions that had originated with the early Fabians in a social environment much different from the one that followed the war. The nationalisation programme, for example, proceeded as if modern industry were not characterised by the separation of ownership and control, and as if effective control could be gained by the simple step of acquiring stock. Similarly, controls over industry seemed to assume that even without scrutiny and vigilance there would still result a correspondence between Government policy and the actual direction of industry, and that regardless of political climate the collaboration of business was assured.

By now, however, it is clear that these assumptions must give way to a theory which can serve as a guide to future action. So far as further nationalisation is concerned, the efficiency test will not sustain the case for nationalisation as industry becomes increasingly modernised, nor does the American experience suggest that continued public support for nationalisation can be founded on the monopoly or ' bigness ' issue. The problem of effective control, of the unification of policy and administration, will become more crucial as the lines between opposing forces are more sharply drawn. It is possible to suggest, therefore, that the Labour Party is in urgent need of a theoretical critique which can serve to generate a new dynamic sufficient to carry its members to the outskirts of the Socialist Commonwealth. No longer can it gain victory by taking a stand against the evils and iniquities of *laisser-faire* capitalism, for they have been largely abolished by the Welfare State. The mixed economy itself is now the point of departure, and it is difficult to imagine any further evolution of socialist politics that does not subject the Welfare State to an analysis as searching as that which the Webbs directed at the capitalism of their day.

It is in this context that the current disturbances within the Labour Party can be understood. The main political challenge to the status quo derives from the rank and file members of the Labour Party, to whom the Welfare State brought material but not spiritual satisfactions. Here it is not difficult to discern a quest for the substance of the vision that has inspired, but has always eluded, the Socialist movement everywhere.

Once again, the Labour Party must reformulate its basic principles. Nor is there much time to lose. ' There are constellations in history ', Karl Mannheim wrote in 1945,

' in which certain possibilities have their chance, and if they

are missed the opportunity may well be gone for ever. Just
as the revolutionary waits for his hour, the reformer whose
concern it is to remould society by peaceful means must
seize his passing chance.'[1]

[1] Karl Mannheim, *Diagnosis of Our Time* (New York, 1944), p. viii.

Schedule of Advisors and Directors of Commodity Divisions of the Ministry of Food as of February 26, 1946.

Position	Name	Paid or Unpaid	Firm connection
A Advisors :			
Commercial	Sir John Bodinnar	Unpaid	C. & T. Harris, Ltd.
General Trade	Sir Henry Ridpath	,,	Ridpath Bros., Ltd.
Alcohol and Yeast	Hugh Paul	,,	Albion Sugar Co.
Cereal Products	J. Maclean	,,	Thos. Borthwick, Ltd.
Manufactured Foods	H. Jephcott	,,	Glaxo, Ltd.
Milk	J. K. Murdock	,,	Unknown
	W. A. Nell	,,	Express Dairy, Ltd.
	G. Walworth	,,	Co-operative Union
	F. J. Burns Reid	,,	Scottish Milk Trades Fed.
	M. B. Rowlands	,,	United Dairies, Ltd.
B Directors :			
Animal Feeding Stuffs	H. R. Humphreys	Paid	Lever Bros. and Unilever
Bacon and Ham	J. London	Unpaid	John London & Co., Ltd.
Bakery	W. H. Philips	Paid	Huntley & Palmers, Ltd.
Canned Fish	A. S. Warren	Unpaid	Warren & Reynolds, Ltd.
Canned Fruit and Vegetables	B. E. Payne	,,	Joseph Travers and Sons, Ltd.
Cereal Products	C. A. Loombe	Unpaid	Reckitt & Colman, Ltd.
Coffee and Cocoa	E. R. Greene	Paid	Brazilian Warrant Co., Ltd.
Cold Storage	J. A. Robertson	Paid	Lightfoot Refrigerating Co., Ltd.
Dehydration (also fish, oils and fats)	J. P. Van den Bergh	Unpaid	Lever Bros. and Unilever
Dried Fruits and edible nuts	J. J. Scouter	Paid	Unknown
Eggs	J. A. Peacock	Unpaid	Nurden & Peacock, Ltd.
Freight (also warehousing)	L. W. Phillips	Unpaid	T. A. Jones and Co.
Fresh fruits and vegetables	C. H. Lewis	Paid	E. H. Lewis & Son, Ltd.
Fruit and vegetable products	G. T. Shipston	Paid	California Fruit Growers Exchange, Ltd.
Imported cereals	J. V. Rank	Unpaid	Joseph Rank, Ltd.
Manufactured foods	F. W. Aldridge	,,	Co-operative Wholesale Society, Ltd.
Meat and Livestock	Sir Henry Turner	Paid	New Zealand Refrigerating Co., Ltd.
	J. C. Kidd	,,	Penrith Farmers and Kidd Auction Co., Ltd.
	H. Jones	,,	W. Weddell & Co., Ltd.
Milk Products	J. W. Rodden	Unpaid	Unknown
Oils and fats	J. W. Knight	,,	United Africa Co. (Unilever)
Potatoes and carrots	Sir John Mollett	Paid	Unknown
Retail Co-ordination	A. Greig	Unpaid	Allied Supplies, Ltd.

Appendix I

Position	*Name*	*Paid or Unpaid*	*Firm connection*
Rice	H. L. Sanderson	Unpaid	Charles Wimble Sons & Co.
Starch	J. Roberts	Paid	Reckitt & Colman, Ltd.
Sugar	Sir William Rook	Unpaid	C. Czarnikow, Ltd.
Tea	Henry Jones	,,	Ewart MacCaughey & Co., Ltd.
Transport	A. G. Marsden	,,	Cadbury & Fry
Wholesale	C. Eustace Davies	Paid	H. H. & So. Budgett & Co., Ltd.

(Source : *Hansard,* Cols. 293-294, February 26, 1946).

APPENDIX II

In 1947 the Federation of British Industries was represented on the following Government committees :

Committee	*No. of Representatives*
Economic Planning Board	3
National Production Advisory Council on Industry	7
Emergency Committee	3
Raw Materials Sub-Committee	3
Regional Boards for Industry . ...?	37
Board of Trade :	
Census of Production Committee	1
Committee on Export Forms	3
Consultative Committee for Industry	4
Colonial Office :	
Economic Research Committee	1
Ministry of Civil Aviation :	
National Civil Aviation Consultative Committee	1
Ministry of Education :	
Regional Councils for Further Education	8
Regional Advisory Committees for Higher Technical Education	2
Regional Academic Boards	1
Ministry of Fuel and Power:	
Industrial Coal Consumers' Council	3
Ministry of Health :	
Central Advisory Water Committee	2
Prevention of Pollution Sub-Committee	1
Water Softening Sub-Committee	1
Sub-Committee on Land Drainage Legislation	1
Scottish Advisory Committee on Rivers Pollution Prevention	1
Ministry of Labour :	
Appointments Department Advisory Council	1
Ministry of Transport :	
Winter Transport Executive	1
Department of Scientific Research :	
Advisory Council on Scientific Policy	1
Technical Information Services Sub-Committee of Research and Productivity Committee	1
Total number of Ministries and Departments	10
Total number of Committees	37
Total number of representations	87

(Source : 31st *Annual Report*, 1947)

APPENDIX III

Leadership in the Federation of British Industries, 1950

Position	Name	Business connections, professional background, etc.
President	Sir Robert Sinclair	British American Tobacco Imperial Tobacco
Deputy-President	Sir Archibald Forbes	Spillers (Flour)
Past President	Sir Clive Baillieu	Midland Bank, Dunlop, mining
	Sir Frederick Bain	Imperial Chemical Industries, Royal Assurance
	Lord Barnby	Director of 18 companies, mainly in textile manufacturing
	Sir George Beharrell	Dunlop
	Sir Peter Bennett	Imperial Chemical Industries, Lloyds Bank, Member of Parliament
	Lord Ebbisham	Blades, East and Blades, Ltd. (printers)
	Lieut.-Col. Lord Dudley Gordon	Barclays Bank, Phoenix Assurance
	Sir Francis Joseph	Lloyds Bank, Midland Bank, collieries, Birmingham Small Arms
	Sir James Lithgow	Director of 23 companies, mainly investment banking, Iron and Steel Federation
	Sir George Nelson	English Electric, Marconi Wireless
Vice-Presidents	Lord Aberconway	Collieries, banking, Insurance, iron and steel
	Mr. Henry Allcock	
	Sir Harold Bowden	Lloyds, cycles
	Sir Ernest R. Canning	W. Canning Co., Ltd. (Engineering
	Mr. Clive Cookson	Coal, iron, insurance
	Mr. F. R. M. de Paula	Banking, business machines, gramophones
	Sir Bernard Docker	Midland Bank, insurance, tramways)
	Mr. Arthur Dorman	Iron and steel, coal
	Mr. George Garnett	Insurance, textiles
	Mr. E. W. Goodale	Textiles, trade association posts
	Sir Patrick Hannon	Director of 19 companies, president British-Latin American Chamber of Commerce, National Union of Manufacturers
	Mr. Forest Hewit	Trade association posts
	Mr. L. J. E. Hooper	Pottery
	Mr. Alexander Johnston	North British Rubber Co.
	Lt.-Col. Sir Cyril James	Insurance
	Sir Guy Locock	Insurance
	Sir William Clare Lees	Insurance, banking
	Colonel R. K. Morcom	Lloyds, iron and steel
	Viscount Nuffield	Nuffield Organisation (Automobiles)
	Sir Roland Nugent	Speaker of the Senate, Northern Ireland
	Mr. R. Paltridge	
	Sir Alexander Roger	Midland, telephones, cables
	Sir Charles Tennyson	Dunlop Rubber
	Sir Evan Williams	Collieries, iron and steel, Lloyds.

INDEX